Also by Ashleigh Renard:
Swing

Published by MW Books, an imprint of Manitoba Woman Media, LLC.

For more information please contact:

pr@manitobawomanmedia.com
www.ashleighrenard.com

ISBN 978-1-7365968-0-7 (paperback)

First edition

Cover and layout design: Sar Dugan (www.sardugan.com)

Cover photo and author photo: Candy Hoehn of SugaShoc Photography

MW
BOOKS

KEEPING IT HOT

THE WORKBOOK

For anyone who's felt that life should be easier.

TABLE OF CONTENTS

INTRODUCTION

HOW THIS BOOK CAME TO BE

In 2019, I left my life as a figure skating coach and choreographer to finally "write my book." I had always planned to be an author, but figure skating has a way of taking over your life, kind of like a forest fire, leaving little time and few resources for anything else.

As a young athlete and an early adopter of perfectionism, I learned to keep going even when my body and mind screamed no. I believed this made me disciplined and mature (which is not entirely incorrect), but I realized ten years and three kids into my marriage that a lifetime of ignoring the signals from my body and mind had led to burnout, overwhelm, and disconnection.

My first book, *Swing*, is the story of how I rehabbed my shabby marriage through a long and arduous process of renegotiating my relationship with myself. *Swing* was published in 2021 and was an instant success. My online community grew rapidly, and I currently reach eight million people each week through short videos in which I offer insights on marriage and parenting. My most popular videos series are "How to Keep Monogamy Hot," "Before You Get a Divorce," and "How to Get Your Kids to Clean the House" (because nothing makes me prouder than child labor).

I write a members-only newsletter where I share weekly inspiration and exclusive video content for couples looking to improve their relationships (and singles who want to raise the bar for new relationships). For more information on Keeping it Hot: The Community, scan here.

For those who know they want to implement satisfying and lasting change in their relationships right freaking now, I offer group coaching programs where I help clients implement the ideas outlined in this book and get clear on what they want and how to get it.

For more information about my group coaching programs, scan here.

HOW TO USE THIS BOOK

From my own experience of coaching teams and learning to nurture myself and based on my interactions with thousands of couples who have reached out to me online, I truly believe our relationships with others can only be as healthy as the relationship we have with ourselves. So, you might be wondering, why did I write a book about improving intimacy with your partner?

Establishing new habits and shaking off our conditioning is hard. The resistance, fear, and apathy that arise can easily make change feel impossible. But, because focusing on sex offers the possibility of immediate results[1], it is a good place to start.

Figuring out what you want in life and how to get it can feel impossible if your closest relationships are out of harmony. When the people closest to you want more from you, but you are not getting what you need from

---

[1] Helping you determine your sexual orientation or asexuality is beyond the scope of this book or my experience, but you can find resources here : https://www.thetrevorproject.org/ and https://www.asexuality.org/.

them, it can seem impossible to expand toward satisfaction in any other area of your life. You might find yourself thinking, *How could I possibly achieve more joy, abundance, and connection, when I can't even figure out how to have a happy marriage or family?*

This book invites you to consider that starting with the goal of spicing up physical intimacy may be the easiest gateway into the self-awareness needed to know what you want, and how to ask for it, in every area of your life. Improved communication, cooperation, and fulfillment across the board? Yes, please.

It starts with ideas on how to mix things up in the bedroom, and moves into self-awareness exercises to help you get clear on what you really need to feel satisfied — beyond what you think you *should* need, or what the world implies you deserve. Regardless of gender, sexual orientation, geography, or culture, we are each unique, mysterious creatures, and no two of us are likely to be satisfied by the same things.

One of the biggest difficulties of adulting is the pull (real and imagined) that everybody and everything must be taken care of before we can take care of ourselves. Throughout this book you'll find blank pages asking: *What's on your mind?* I invite you to use these to brain dump any thoughts that don't relate to the subject at hand. Need toilet paper? Must call in a prescription refill? Have to return overdue library books? Got something you forgot to tell a team member at work? Dump it all on these pages so you can stay in the moment while doing these exercises.

You may be wondering: *Do I need my partner to work through this book with me?* Nope! You can proceed entirely on your own and not even tell your partner. Or you can each get a copy and compare worksheets every night. Or take a screenshot of a page and ask your partner how they would answer. You can do whatever the hell you want. It's your book, your rules.

You do not need anyone's permission or participation to change and learn and grow. You do not need your partner to work through this book with you for your relationship to transform. Even if you do work through the book together, ideally you'll do each exercise privately so you can really be honest with your thoughts.

I hope this book acts as a giant permission slip to start understanding your uniqueness more deeply, and I hope it provides communication strategies and cooperation hacks to help you raise the bar in your relationships. The exercises in this book offer strategies and answers, but I hope more than anything they will offer new questions for you to ask yourself and your partner.

I am so happy you are here, truly.

Massive love,

Ashleigh

If you feel unsafe in your relationship or family,
please know there is help and love and support for you.

https://www.thetrevorproject.org/get-help/

https://www.thehotline.org/

PART ONE

WARMUPS: 10 THINGS THAT ARE NOT SEX THAT CAN GET YOU IN THE MOOD FOR SEX

1. Make a sexy playlist.

2. Wash your favorite lingerie, or order new lingerie.

3. Put candles in the bedroom (don't forget matches or a lighter).

4. Put a drop of a great fragrance or essential oil on your bed linens.

5. Watch something sexy, alone or together.

6. Listen to an erotic audio story.

7. Wash and charge your favorite bedroom electronic.

8. Order in, intentionally. Get your favorite takeout, set the table, and eat like you are out on a date. No phones, no distractions.

9. Take a half hour to do the bodyscaping and hygiene that makes you feel sexy.

10. Move your body for twenty minutes. Roll out your yoga mat. Take a jog around the block. Leave your phone at home. Move. Breathe.

HOT SEX IS JUST
THE TIP OF THE ICEBERG

Instructions: Color in each supporting statement you agree with below the iceberg in this illustration to get a baseline of your level of comfort and fulfillment right at this moment. We will revisit it as we make our way through the book.

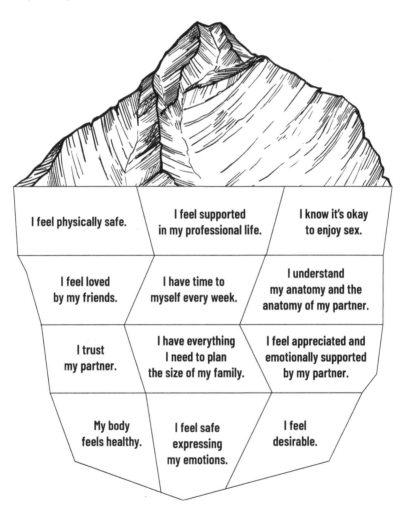

I feel physically safe.

I feel supported in my professional life.

I know it's okay to enjoy sex.

I feel loved by my friends.

I have time to myself every week.

I understand my anatomy and the anatomy of my partner.

I trust my partner.

I have everything I need to plan the size of my family.

I feel appreciated and emotionally supported by my partner.

My body feels healthy.

I feel safe expressing my emotions.

I feel desirable.

Often, the focus in a relationship is on whether sex is happening and whether it is good. But even if hot sex is happening, if the other areas are depleted, emotional intimacy and trust will not be secure. Having hot sex at the beginning of your relationship holds little weight when you are further into the reality of holding down an adult relationship on Planet Earth.

Oh, but we had great sex when we just met. Um, yeah, I'm sure you did.[2] Bonding hormones and endorphins will create that chemistry and attraction, but when you start sailing the ocean of real life, we need to take a look at what is beneath the surface.

Ideally, satisfying intimacy is a side effect of a healthy and compatible partnership.

It's unlikely anyone will have every segment filled in. If you experience chronic pain or disability, the "my body feels healthy" statement will have to be assessed relative to the most comfort you can realistically expect considering your physical state. If you are struggling with trying to conceive, emotional and financial issues may complicate your ability to enjoy sex.

Now, let's consider whether hot sex could be the catalyst for fulfillment in these other areas. What if getting clear on what you want, and knowing how to ask for and get it could lead to satisfaction in other aspects of your life?

KEEPING IT HOT: TIPS

 Figure out your favorite time of day to have sex.

In our house, nighttime is for sleeping and mornings are for coffee, so our preferred time for sex is 5:30 p.m. How do we accomplish this with kids, you ask? Screen time. If they are playing video games, they are not interested in where we are or what we are doing. We lock the bedroom door, turn on the sound machine, and toss the sex blanket over the bed. (More on that in a second.)

---

[2] By the way, if sex was something that took time to figure out, that is cool, too.

2 Get a sex blanket.

We have a lightweight, tight-weave blanket that is used only for intimacy. We throw it over our made bed so we can fully enjoy the sensations of body oil and lube without worrying about staining our sheets or duvet cover.

3 Put a mirror across from your bed.

Whether you like to watch yourself giving, receiving, or both (neither is okay, too!), having the option to watch adds a whole new dimension to the experience.

4 Bring electronics into the bedroom.

I'm not talking about humidifiers and a new clock radio. I'm talking toys. Our faves are the Magic Wand (formerly Hitachi), the Wild Rose suction vibrator, and the Fleshlight Turbo.

> "Ever since I took your advice on introducing toys in the bedroom, our sex life has been amazing. And it has awakened so much more excitement between my husband and myself."
>
> Marcy (she/her)

5 Get turned on, but don't do it.

Try reading or listening to something sexy a couple times a day, but don't act on it. Raise your baseline for arousal and see how it shifts your mood throughout the day.

"You mentioned reading or listening to sexy stories. I started writing them. I don't share them, even with the hubby, but these little stories help put me in the mood and give me something to think about when I am bored or overwhelmed. It makes me feel sexy and more confident for whatever reason, and he notices, which leads to more sexy time."

Chelsea (she/her)

Try double penetration (DP).

DP usually refers to vaginal and anal insertion at the same time, and the resulting feeling of fullness is a sensation that can be enjoyable. It can also refer to fingers inserted along with a penis or toy, or a toy inserted with a penis. With electronics, clean hands, lots of lube, and a little imagination, there are endless options for both partners. Go slow. Take cues from your partner — or, if you're the recipient, give your partner feedback. And have fun exploring each other's bodies in new ways.

"Your tip about adding a finger/s during penetration. We've used it during spooning position to GREAT success. Coupled with the usual thrusting and a suction vibrator toy, it's incredible!"

Scott (he/him)

7 Try oral only.

This brought about the biggest change in our routine. After our third baby was born, we were certain we didn't want to conceive again. We were also at a standstill for what to do about birth control. He didn't want to have a vasectomy and I didn't want to go back on hormonal birth control. Neither of us was motivated to push the other toward compromise, so we came up with our own creative solution. For ten days every month (five days before ovulation and five days after) we decided we would do things other than intercourse.[3] For us, that includes some toy play and a lot of oral, usually back and forth, switching each time the other gets close to orgasm. Whatever you do all the time, try not doing that for a day, a week, or a whole month, and see what other activities you find to fill its place.

8 Take a time out.

Unless we are having a super-quick quickie, we always practice edging. We naturally did it for years, solo and together, before we realized there was a term for it. We both thought, *wait, isn't that just called good sex?* When you are getting close to climax, switch up what you are doing to prolong the experience and let the sensation build.

9 Add more solo playtime to your routine.

Instead of thinking of masturbation as a thing to do if you're not having sex or instead of sex, what if it led to more intimacy with your partner? Try giving each other space once a week to have a shower or bath and the bedroom to yourself. Watch, read, or listen to something sexy to get yourself turned on. And see if it leads to an increase in satisfaction when you are together.

---

[3] We use the withdrawal method at all other times of the month and we both prefer it to him ejaculating inside. The only time in our relationship when we didn't use withdrawal were the three periods when we were actively trying to conceive — eight months in 2006, four months in 2008, and twenty minutes in 2012. For more information on the effectiveness of the withdrawal method when used by a responsible ejaculator, please consult your healthcare professional.

"I grew up in church and youth group. I was taught chastity was the way God intended it. I still am a follower of Jesus and do believe the Bible teaches sex is for marriage. Since getting married, I've still felt the shame I was taught around sex and masturbation. Finding your *Keeping It Hot* posts and being encouraged by your stories and activities has opened up so much more discussion for my husband and me. Most importantly, it has made me comfortable with sexual desire and given me permission to explore solo and as a couple."

Rachel (she/her)

 Ask questions.

Bodies and preferences can change, so get in the habit of asking your partner what feels good. Start with trying two different things and asking an either/or question in the moment. "Does it feel better like this or like this?"

When trying something new, don't expect to get it exactly right the first time. It may take practice. And, if you are bringing in a new electronic, I recommend experimenting with it solo for a week or so before bringing it into partner play. Figuring out how to use something new is always harder for me if I have someone watching over my shoulder. Having someone between my legs would make it almost impossible. 😂

Instructions: Take a break and ask yourself, would you rather:

Have a monthly hotel date night?

Have a monthly two-hour hike with your partner?

THIS OR THAT?

What made you choose your answer?

_____

_____

_____

_____

_____

_____

_____

_____

_____

_____

_____

_____

_____

_____

_____

_____

_____

_____

_____

_____

_____

_____

_____

Make a connection. Take a picture and share with a loved one!

What do they think? Start a conversation.

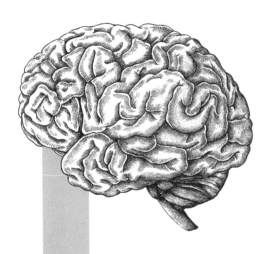

WHAT'S ON YOUR MIND?

PART TWO

Since publishing *Swing*, I have heard over and over that couples have used the stories in that book as fodder for some hot bedroom activities. Here is an example that took place in a car, not a bedroom.

"Last month, my wife and I went on a trip with some friends of ours and rented a cabin for the weekend. My wife and I had just started reading your book but hadn't actually read it together. It was a three-hour drive to our cabin, so we decided to listen to the audio version together. Listening to your stories got both of us extremely hot. Neither one of us could keep our hands off each other. Knowing that our friends were already at the cabin waiting on us, we couldn't take it anymore. I pulled off the highway and found a secluded area near a river. My wife and I got married when we were really young, still in college. We have been together for ten years now and married for nine. We joked because we haven't done anything like that since we were just dating. After we did our thing we got back on the road and continued listening to the audiobook. We finally made it to our cabin and of course were the last couple to arrive."

Matt (he/him) and Tess (she/her)

If I had to guess, I'd say Matt and Tess were listening to Chapter 4. 😄

But would you believe that most of the messages I receive have nothing to do with sex?

Instead, they are stories about how *Swing* inspired them to get clear on what they really wanted and find the courage to start new conversations, or revisit old ones (you know, the ones that always end in a stalemate?) in a new way.

KEEPING THE PEACE IS NOT PEACEFUL AT ALL. IT SHOULD BE CALLED "MAINTAINING AN INCREDIBLE LEVEL OF AWKWARDNESS."

Make it your own. Color, write, or draw and share with our community!

@ashleighrenard | #KeepingItHot

So, I wasn't surprised when I continued reading the message from Matt and Tess, and they shared what happened in the car ride home after that mountain weekend.

"We had a great kid-free weekend with our friends. Sunday arrives, and we start to head back. We continue to listen to your audiobook on the way home. We picked up where we left off, but this time it was way different. My wife pauses the audio and starts asking some pretty serious questions about our relationship. She was telling me things I had no idea she had felt, and I shared things she had no idea about, either. She really took me by surprise when she told me that she feels like I'm not in love with her anymore. I assured her that even though we've had some rough times in our marriage, I've never fallen out of love with her. It broke my heart that my wife felt that way and I had no idea. It made me realize that we have been going through the motions for much of our relationship. Since this trip, my wife and I have been stronger than ever. We both continue to follow your stories on Instagram and can't wait for your next book."

In my experience, nothing will get you to a new place faster than saying the thing you think you can never, ever say.

But what if you have been censoring your thoughts and feelings for so long that you don't really know what you want or what you really want to say? If so, you've come to the right place (okay, the right book). Getting down to the awkward, honest fact of the matter is (weirdly) my favorite thing.

Let's get started.

Can figuring out your satisfaction be as easy as 1, 2, 3? My experience as a skating coach and official says yes.

Instructions: You will rate each area of your life based on a 1 – 3 measuring system.

1 below expectations

2 meeting expectations

3 surpassing expectations

I'm talking about **your expectations** for your one wild, precious life. Not what someone else thinks is good enough. This is a check-in with your heart: *Are these things where I want them to be?*

That's it. But here's the caveat: **You cannot give half scores.** If you are thinking, *well, it's a little below my expectations, but not quite a one,* I need to tell you: **It's a one.**

If you're thinking, *well, it's a little above my expectations, but not fully a three,* my babe, **it's a two.**

For something to be a three, in my book it needs to be a wow.

Take a deep breath. Now begin. Check off the first number that comes to mind for each.

Singles: skip the partner questions or substitute with someone else you are close to.

Need more room? Get half-price digital worksheets here.

LIFE ASSESSMENT

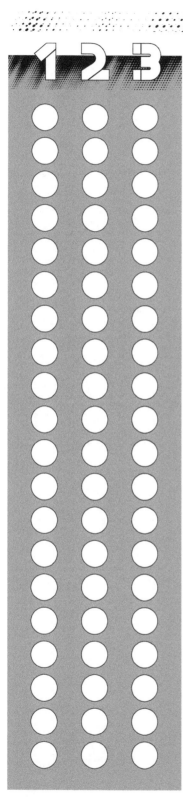

My physical health

My mental health

My nutrition

The amount of money I have

The way I spend my money

The amount of time I have to myself

Quality of my activity when I have time to myself

How well my partner hears me

My partner's openness and honesty with me

How appreciated I feel by my partner

How well I appreciate my partner

The individual relationship I have with child 1

The individual relationship I have with child 2

The individual relationship I have with child 3

Systems that help me feel supported at home

Systems that help me feel supported at work

How much I can count on my friends

How often I laugh

How often I feel adventurous

How often I feel inspired

Imagine if you were a three in each section, how would you feel as you woke up each morning? How would your surroundings be different? How would you drink your coffee? How would you move through your day?

Instructions: Use your five senses to describe these imagined scenes.

My physical health:

_____
_____
_____
_____
_____
_____

My mental health:

_____
_____
_____
_____
_____

My nutrition:

_____
_____
_____
_____
_____
_____

The amount of money I have:

_____

_____

_____

_____

_____

The way I spend my money:

_____

_____

_____

_____

_____

The amount of time I have to myself:

_____

_____

_____

_____

_____

Quality of my activity when I have time to myself:

_____

_____

_____

_____

_____

How well my partner hears me:

My partner's openness and honesty with me:

How appreciated I feel by my partner:

How well I appreciate my partner:

The individual relationship I have with child 1:

_____
_____
_____
_____
_____
_____

The individual relationship I have with child 2:

_____
_____
_____
_____
_____
_____

The individual relationship I have with child 3:

_____
_____
_____
_____
_____
_____

Systems that help me feel supported at home:

_____
_____
_____
_____
_____

Systems that help me feel supported at work:

_____
_____
_____
_____

How much I can count on my friends:

_____
_____
_____
_____
_____

How often I laugh:

_____
_____
_____
_____

How often I feel adventurous:

_____
_____
_____
_____

How often I feel inspired:

_____
_____
_____
_____

FROM *SWING*

If you had difficulty tapping into how you felt about any of those areas, you are not alone. During our lifetimes, many of us learn to disconnect from our intuition and push down our emotions. I learned this in figure skating.

I was two years old the first time my parents laced me into skates. By elementary school, I was on the ice five days a week. In the early mornings, the world still lit by moonlight, I rolled from my warm bed already wearing my skating clothes — a time-saver my mom insisted upon. She and I padded quietly through the darkened house. We turned on no lights, save one mounted under the upper cupboards of the kitchen, which remained on all night to avoid waking the rest of the family. Cereal boxes and bowls sat on the kitchen table, laid out the night before. The room was filled with the smell of coffee. My mom took hers black in a tall aluminum travel mug, with two ice cubes, rinsed under the tap before being dropped in the coffee and dissolving quickly. In just a few hours my mom would rinse the filter and fill it again with grounds, pouring water from a plastic pitcher until it reached the max fill line, resetting the coffee maker for the next morning.

The frigid air struck me only briefly as I dashed to the warm car. My mom joined me after unplugging the extension cord from the block heater, the cord of which flopped out from under the car hood all winter long. The drive took two minutes. The soles of my feet were still tight from sleep as I walked methodically over the thickly packed snow of the rink parking lot, rolling from heel to toe, letting each icy peak massage away the sleepiness through the soles of my heavy Sorels. My hands stuffed deep in my pockets and my shoulders high to cover my ears with the collar of my parka, I shifted my feet back and forth as my mom unlocked the door. The key was on its own ring, slung through a roughly drilled hole in a slice of thick, white plastic left over from the dismantling of the old rink boards. I was familiar with the persistent coolness of the plastic, the way my fingers felt when I ran them perpendicularly over the grooves and slices permanently etched on it. I knew this key, but I wasn't sure if we possessed a key to our own house. I carried nothing — everything I needed was kept inside the locker room, which in just a few minutes would be warmed in equal measure by space heaters and the exuberant chatter of pre-teens who cared not that the clock had yet to strike 7 a.m.

Each day began with forty-five minutes of figures. We called it "patch" because we each chose a section of clean ice on which to practice our patterns. Over and over, the rink silent and the lights bright, we traced figure eights. Forward and backward, and with turns as we advanced, it was my favorite part of training. Some of my friends skated haphazardly over their own patches, impatient to practice their jumps and spins, but I was in no rush. My patch was meticulous.

On test days, heavy-booted judges stood on the ice to watch us skate our figures, each pattern traced thrice before completion. Without fail, at least one of them squatted down close to the ice to wipe away snow with a sheepskin-lined leather mitten. This is the world's most perfect mitten. No other style could keep a hand warmer nor compete with the volume of applause generated when they were clapped together. The latter attribute motivated me, before every high school hockey game, to dig as relentlessly as a terrier to find a matching pair in the storage compartment mounted under the deacon's bench at our front door.

The judge wiped away the snow to see my tracings more clearly. They were looking for flats. As I watched their assessment of my work, I silently prayed that they wouldn't find them. Flats were bad. A flat's presence on the ice divulged that my body lean had been weak and weight placement on the blade incorrect, resulting in two shallow, parallel lines. As the judge crouched lower, their widening knees threatening to pop the zipper on their full-length parka, I hoped they'd see only single, deep grooves on the ice, indicating that I maintained a true edge around each figure eight and on the entry and exit of each turn. I appreciated the simple integrity of being assessed based on the prints my blade left on the ice. A tracing does not lie.

A landed jump may be considered better by some if it's higher or if the flow across the ice is maintained on the landing edge. A figure tracing, on the other hand, was an inalterable record of performance, the perfection of which was directly proportional to the focus employed. It was one part story, telling the tale of the balance over the blade, and it was one part math — a correctly laid out and executed equation.

I have one flat that I'll carry with me forever, carved accidentally into the skin covering the medial edge of my gastrocnemius. It, and the other sixteen visible scars on my left leg, was the result of a habitually poorly placed free leg on the takeoff of my double Salchows. Oftentimes, I grazed my leg with my right blade and briefly thought I had escaped injury because my tights were not torn. Most often, I was reminded of the truth I learned too young: human flesh is more tender than any manmade material. I pinched my two layers of Mondor tights and plucked them away from my skin, breath suspended as I waited for a count of three.

If a growing scarlet patch did not appear, I set up for another double Sal. If blood did appear, I retreated to the locker room, pulling my dress and tights down to my ankles, dress inside out and draped like a splayed chicken over my still-tied skates. I dabbed the cut with a tissue and covered it with bandages, one to three depending on the size of the wound, all the while my head upside down, nose running due to the temperature change, mucus pooling in the top curve of my nostrils with an excruciating tickle. I'd pull up my dress, wipe my nose, and return to the ice in my blood-stained tights. Of the seventeen cuts that left scars, the flat is my favorite. The rest were small, some merely nicks. Many were originally deep, but this one was long.

On the day of the injury, it measured three inches, slicing clean through my double layer of tights, which gaped instantly, framing the cut like labia. Two tiny rivulets of blood sprang from the skin, running parallel until they pooled together in my boot, the skin between the incisions pink and pulsing, astonished that it remained untouched. Even in scar form, both edges remained clearly shown over its full length, a perfect flat. It puzzled me afterwards, seemingly impossible that I contorted my foot into the dorsiflexion required to brand myself in this way. But a tracing does not lie.

I didn't have to wait for test days or competitions to stand on the ice as the judges displayed their scores. I could appraise myself each day.

Perfectly shaped figure eights, tracings all within an inch of each other, each new pattern set up one blade's length from the last. Years of report cards with straight A's. A stack of notebooks, holding a decade of records, calories in and calories out, reps and sets completed, miles run, food allowances, weight-loss goals. Collectively, a memoir of my discipline, assurance that I was living a correctly laid out and executed life.

Some may say perfection is unattainable, but figure skaters know different. Every day we ventured closer to the inevitable. There would be a time when all the work, the early mornings, the bruises upon bruises that created a spectacle of color that put most canvases to shame, the steam rising from our sweaty heads as our toes turned a buttery yellow from the cold resulted in a performance that struck all who were watching as both effortless and beautiful. It would be declared, "Yes, you did it. It was perfect, and everyone likes you."

We would be awarded the 6.0.

Need more room? Get half-price digital worksheets here.

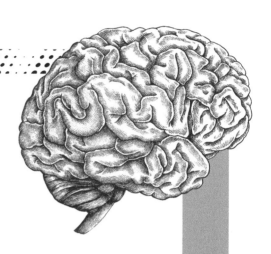

WHAT'S ON YOUR MIND?

Instructions: Take a break and ask yourself, would you rather:

Your partner surprise you with a new toy?

Your partner surprise you with a new outfit?

THIS OR THAT?

What made you choose your answer?

_____
_____
_____
_____
_____
_____
_____
_____
_____
_____
_____
_____
_____
_____
_____
_____
_____
_____
_____
_____
_____
_____
_____
_____
_____

Make a connection. Take a picture and share with a loved one!

What do they think? Start a conversation.

Instructions: Ask yourself these three questions.

1 What do I need more of?

_____
_____
_____
_____
_____
_____
_____
_____

2 What do I need less of?

_____
_____
_____
_____
_____
_____
_____
_____

3 What do I need clarity around?

_____
_____
_____
_____
_____
_____
_____
_____

QUESTIONS AND SCENARIOS

Instructions: Describe the following scenario with both the actions you'd take and the feelings you'd feel.

IF NO ONE WAS JUDGING ME I WOULD:

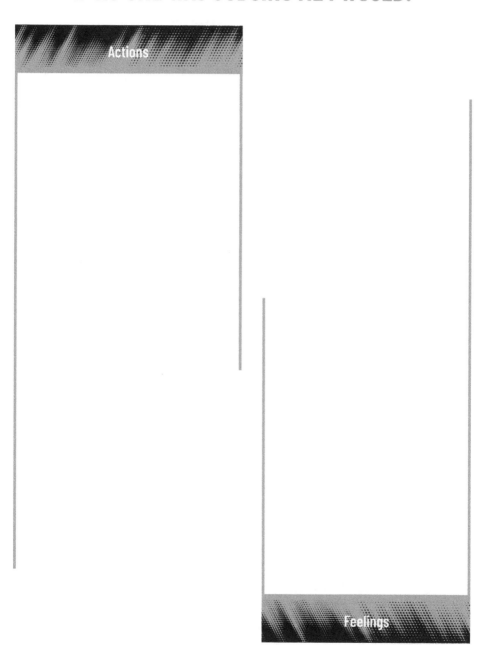

Actions

Feelings

Instructions: Get your creative juices flowing and draw the same scenario with both the actions you'd take and the feelings you'd feel from the previous page.

IF NO ONE WAS JUDGING ME I WOULD:

Make a connection. Take a picture and share with a loved one!

What do they think? Start a conversation.

Instructions: Describe the following scenario with both the actions you'd take and the feelings you'd feel.

WITH LIMITLESS TIME I WOULD:

Actions

Feelings

Instructions: Get your creative juices flowing and draw the same scenario with both the actions you'd take and the feelings you'd feel from the previous page.

WITH LIMITLESS TIME I WOULD:

Make a connection. Take a picture and share with a loved one!

What do they think? Start a conversation.

Instructions: Describe the following scenario with both the actions you'd take and the feelings you'd feel.

WITH LIMITLESS RESOURCES I WOULD:

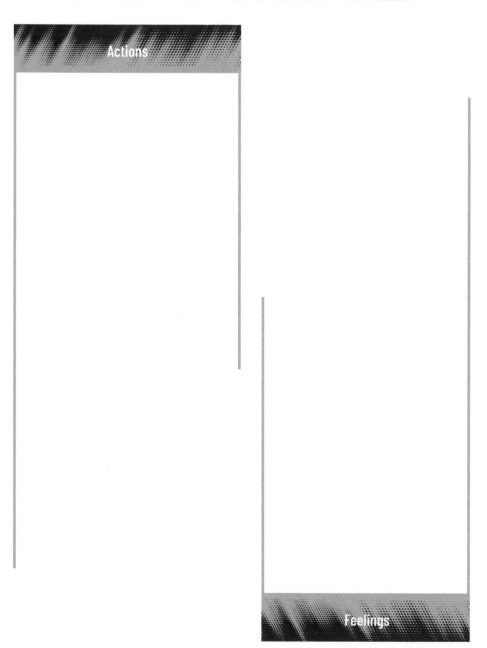

Actions

Feelings

Instructions: Get your creative juices flowing and draw the same scenario with both the actions you'd take and the feelings you'd feel from the previous page.

WITH LIMITLESS RESOURCES I WOULD:

Make a connection. Take a picture and share with a loved one!

What do they think? Start a conversation.

Instructions: Now, look back to your answers on page 42 and pretend they have materialized. Write a thank you note to life for granting these desires.

Dear Life,

Thank you for giving me more...

THANK YOU LETTERS

Dear Life,

Thank you for releasing...

_____
_____
_____
_____
_____
_____
_____
_____
_____
_____
_____
_____
_____
_____
_____
_____
_____
_____
_____
_____
_____
_____
_____
_____
_____
_____
_____
_____

Dear Life,

Thank you for helping me understand...

Instructions: Take a break and ask yourself, would you rather:

Add more oral to your regular repertoire?

Add more mutual full body massages
with your partner?

THIS OR THAT?

What made you choose your answer?

_____
_____
_____
_____
_____
_____
_____
_____
_____
_____
_____
_____
_____
_____
_____
_____
_____
_____
_____
_____
_____
_____
_____
_____
_____
_____

Make a connection. Take a picture and share with a loved one!

What do they think? Start a conversation.

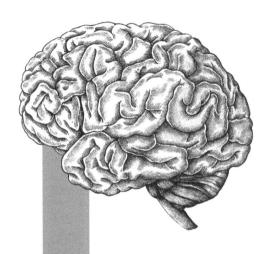

WHAT'S ON YOUR MIND?

PART THREE

ICEBERG, REVISITED

Instructions: Color in each supporting statement below the iceberg to show the fullness you currently feel.

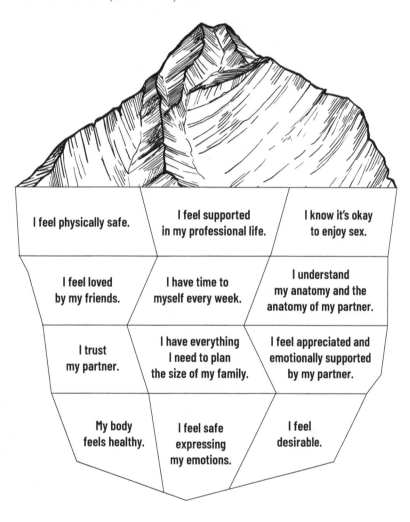

I feel physically safe.

I feel supported in my professional life.

I know it's okay to enjoy sex.

I feel loved by my friends.

I have time to myself every week.

I understand my anatomy and the anatomy of my partner.

I trust my partner.

I have everything I need to plan the size of my family.

I feel appreciated and emotionally supported by my partner.

My body feels healthy.

I feel safe expressing my emotions.

I feel desirable.

EXPERT WEIGH IN FROM
MEGHAN RIORDAN JARVIS, MA, LCSW

Sometimes "Keeping It Hot" means keeping it safe and curious.

Trauma can cause changes in your relationship with your body. Sexual assault, physical and emotional injury, and grief are common drivers of symptoms like fear and pain where there was none before, or even a seemingly absent sex drive. The key to finding a way back to pleasure is by establishing a renewed sense of safety by meeting your body where it is.

The good news is that if you are looking to try and ignite your sex life again, the acute trauma you experienced is in the past. You already survived. Whether it was a physical trauma to your body, like an assault or a surgery, or a natural but unexpected change, such as the loss of a loved one, reclaiming yourself sexually is a beautiful and hopeful act. With a willing partner, sex and intimacy has the potential to heal some of that pain.

The brain responds to trauma by activating a series of instinctive responses known to most of us as fight, flight, and freeze. What is less well known is that *before* we activate that system, we use something called social regulation — in other words, we look around to see who can help. When there isn't a helper, we try to fight, then run away, and if none of that works, we simply try to survive.

As psychiatrist and trauma researcher Bessel Van der Kolk has said, "the body keeps the score." Even though the threat is in the past, the body may be triggered into a present-day state of high reactivity. You may have emotional triggers that require therapeutic work to heal, but the best way to begin stepping back into a *sexual* relationship in a body that has experienced trauma is **to go slow, check in, linger in desire, and don't push.**

Go Slow is exactly what it sounds like. Behave as if your physical body is a new territory. Rather than assuming you have complete command of your turn-ons and likes, remember that your body has changed and is still in recovery. Curiosity is the most important gift to offer. A learner's mind requires a willingness to take your time and get interested in how your body responds to the five-senses experience of sex — touch, sight, sound, smell, and taste. Go slow and be curious.

Checking in sounds a lot like consent, because it is. You may find that it helps to check in with yourself first. Self-stimulation is among the best ways to ease back into your body. Whether you are alone or with someone else, begin by asking your body "how is that for you?" Pause and really listen for a response. Particularly after sexual assault, one move, smell, or word can startle the body back into a protective state that shuts down desire. Go slow and check in to establish safe boundaries.

Linger. Remember how hot all that making out was when you were a teenager? Remember how your face was all chapped and tingly even though you had boundaries on touch? That is the potential that going slow and checking in offers. Have you ever taken a yoga class where the instructor has you hold the stretch so long it hurts? Lingering in desire can offer the same kind of stretch — this time to your body and mind's whole sexual system. Amplifying sexual desire reminds the body of what it is capable of and may possibly reconnect it to pleasurable memories that can lead the body back to itself. Lingering is learning.

Don't push. Pushing implies a predetermined outcome or expectation. It can challenge your sense of safety in the body. Deciding "tonight's the night" doesn't allow for changes in desire and can cause you to inadvertently cross a safety boundary. You don't want to lose the trust and curiosity you have earned by going slow, checking in, and lingering. Don't push yourself.

In most cases, as the body heals, so does your sense of desire. Trauma can drive lots of complicated feelings about being in a body that has changed sexually. If you find that you are spending a lot of time in fear, pain, or judgment, seek support. There are so many wonderful sex therapists who help people re-explore sex, and who offer a series of treatments and techniques to help you expand your sense of safety and confidence and help you reconnect to a meaningful sex life.

Meghan Riordan Jarvis, MA, LCSW, is a psychotherapist specializing in trauma, grief, and loss and works in private practice in Washington, D.C. After experiencing PTSD after the deaths of both of her parents within two years of each other, Meghan started the platform "Grief is My Side Hustle" which includes her popular blog, links to her podcast under the same name, and her free writing workshop, "Grief Mates." Meghan offers public and private sector consultation to leadership teams working to increase emotional fluency and care in decision making and intentional business culture development. Meghan's upcoming memoir, End of the Hour, will be published by Zibby Books.

Need more room? Get half-price digital worksheets here.

Instructions: List all the important people in your life and one word to describe each of them. Try to use the first word that comes to mind.

Person	Word

IMPORTANT PEOPLE

WHEN YOU EXPECT THE WORST FROM PEOPLE, THEY ALWAYS DELIVER.

Make it your own. Color, write, or draw and share with our community!

Instructions: Now look back and ask yourself, are you holding these people in positive regard? How would you really like to feel about them? How would you like to see them? Choose new words to describe them with your new, more positive intentions.

Note: This is not about gaslighting yourself into believing that things are not, in fact, as they are — it's an invitation to consider how this person could bring the most love and joy into your shared experience.

Person	New Words

FROM *SWING*

I continued my lifelong habit of persisting when my body protested and my mind hesitated. Ten years and three kids into my marriage, my body manifested symptoms of this imbalance that were impossible to ignore. I saw more doctors in one year than I had in the previous decade.

I felt sad and frustrated, and more than anything, I wanted to know what I needed to do to get better. And one day in meditation, it came to me: *You need someone who loves you better.*

Uh, okay. So, what does that mean? Does that mean I tell Manny to leave today? Does that mean I leave today? Does that mean I need another boyfriend on the side?

Silence.

How could leaving my marriage possibly be the best thing for my family or for me? The stress and heartache of divorce and dating — how could that bring me greater fulfillment? It couldn't be so. But then why was my intuition telling me I needed to seek a truer, madder, deeper love?

I begged for the answer, and for months I got nothing more than silence. Every morning I would sit, and every morning I would get no closer to understanding. I had never experienced silence in meditation for so long. I tried to hold onto a sliver of hope that I had not lost all connection with a greater guidance and my ability to rely on my intuition.

I felt broken and confused. Beautiful-looking life, continuous mystery ailments, doctor after doctor. What do I do?

You need someone who loves you better.

Do I ask him to move out?

Silence.

Does this mean I should get a divorce?

Silence.

I felt sadder, angrier. Stupid. Helpless. Was this a cop-out, or was not having someone who loved me enough really the root of all my challenges? Was this why it was so hard for me not to yell at my kids? Was this why it was a struggle for me to do the housework with joy? Was this why I felt pulled in two directions with work and family? Was the truth that if I had someone who loved me better this would all be easier?

I had never bought into the "you complete me" phenomenon. I had railed against it since high school. I was probably the only person who disliked the movie, *Jerry Maguire*. As a fifteen-year-old I was like, *You had me at hello?* Blech. *Woman, stand on your own two feet. Please.*

However, I *had* 100 percent bought into the promise of perfection. I had believed that if I controlled everything and lived with enough discipline, life would unfold before me like a yellow brick road. If anything went wrong, someone was surely to blame. Obstacles were a sign that someone had screwed up. I began the work of bringing awareness to these beliefs.

Why would this be coming up? I wanted to be making progress, to be repairing our marriage. I wanted to feel healthy again.

Did I really need someone who loved me better? Maybe I needed more in order to be a whole, healthy person.

I continued to sit — for another six months.

One day I sat in meditation, not thinking this day would be any different from the string of others that had come before. And I heard it again:

You need someone who loves you better.

Yup, I heard you the first hundred times.

It's you.

Huh?

It's you.

Oh. It's me.

It was me.

All this time it had been me.

After months of feeling hopeless and helpless, struggling to see any future vision of my family that was connected and happy, I finally had some guidance. I had my next right step. I had my answer.

And I laughed.

I laughed out loud.

And I cursed the Divine a little through my laughter. Why hadn't I received the message clearly in the first place? I had been listening, after all. Why did it have to take so long and be so confusing? *Next time, would you please make it clearer? And faster? Please?*

Finally, I *had* heard it, and few things excite me more than a new project. And this project was pretty straightforward. I needed to love myself. I needed to love myself better. I needed to love myself maybe for the first time.

I knew immediately how I would do it. I would start with words.

I started writing love letters to myself every day.

At first, they were to me, from me. And some days I wrote several in a row. I offered myself what I felt I needed at that moment: encouragement, love, forgiveness for losing my patience with the boys. I gave myself credit for trying, and permission to rest. Sometimes I told myself that I just looked really pretty. I told myself that my outfit was cute. I assured myself that the intention behind my work with my boys and with my skaters was evident. That my actions were definitely coming from my heart.

Immediately, I felt relief. I felt comfort.

Whenever I had asked Manny for more encouragement or recognition, he had begrudgingly complied for a few days or, more often and more hurtfully, looked at me in a way one looks at a child who has a sundae and is crying for a cherry on top — but has already been given *five* cherries. In other words, as if to say: *Honey, you don't really need what you think you need.* I would feel like I just needed to grow up and stop being so needy.

But through the letters I realized I really did need this kind of support. I wasn't asking for a cherry or even a sundae. I was just asking to be fed.

At the beginning, I made a list of the things I thought would change in our family if I continued the letters to myself, if I continued demanding that we set the bar high for the love expressed in our home. I conservatively predicted that everything would change. I had already seen through my work with [my therapist] that when I changed my way of thinking and relating to others, everything and everyone around me started to change, too. Even if a situation became heated, my responses seemed to flow peacefully, de-escalating the situation instead of making it more explosive. I left confrontations feeling much more grounded than I ever would have in the past, the stress no longer following me around like an aftershock.

I wrote about my wishes for Manny, for each of the boys, and for myself. I imagined us happier, more secure, more comfortable in our own skin, more joyful, and more connected. I imagined Manny less stressed with work. I imagined the tumor in his back causing him less pain. I imagined him talking to me about his day. I imagined the boys cuddling with us more. I imagined us cuddling as a family. I imagined myself healthy. I imagined myself confident in my marriage. I decided to pretend, even if I did not believe it completely, that I was worthy of this kind of family, this kind of love. That we all were.

Why was it that for all these years I had not felt worthy of this love? I felt I needed to be "better" before I loved myself. I felt I needed to accomplish more, complete more, achieve more. If I let up on the pres-

sure, I feared I would stop doing everything I should be doing.
I feared that I was lazy to my core, and the only reason I took on all
I did was to prove my worth. I needed to start exploring just how much
love and encouragement I needed. I had been so hard on myself. For
years I had restricted food and enjoyment. And when I kicked that,
I focused on restricting affirmation and rest.

Was it that I thought succeeding at marriage and parenting and a
professional life were so much harder without love and affection and
validation from myself, and so achieving the former without the latter
made me even tougher, even more accomplished?

I had desperately hoped that each new achievement, the next project
around the house, the next garden harvest, would yield some sort of
affirmation from Manny. I fished for compliments, for confirmation that
I was doing a good job. He could smell the fishing from a mile away, but
often would not indulge me. Why? Did it feel like I was exerting some
sort of control? Did he want affirmation, too, but also felt unworthy or
tougher because he didn't "need" them? He got praise from his mom by
the ton, but never from his dad. Did he just feel that women encourage
people while men sit silent? Did he think that to engage in affection or
encouragement was a sign of weakness, of neediness?

And there we were with our three kiddos — soft, love-searching,
encouragement-needing kiddos. How were we to support them? Was
it enough for me to shower them with praise and affection while they
gazed longingly at their father, who seemed to have a very limited quota
of affection that he could allot each day? The boys had started to brush
off my attention like it was patronizing. After all, if affection was really
something boys could indulge in, wouldn't they be getting it from Manny,
too? Why would they have to beg for it? If you have to beg, is it really
worth it?

Had Manny's cultural conditioning really trained him to ignore the sound
of a woman's voice? Was he too shut down emotionally to ever offer me
the support I needed? Would I always have to start our conversations
with an update on my current proximity to divorce for him to listen?

I didn't know for sure. As I wrote the letters to myself, the fear of being too needy, of pushing for what I wanted in our family, dissipated. I felt braver. I realized that every time I took on a new project, a new goal, a new venture, I hoped to receive admiration from someone, anyone. And often I did.

But admiration is not the same as love. Admiration comes and goes. What I wanted was a love that stayed. And I knew that to give or receive that love, I had to know that I deserved it. I had to love myself unconditionally. I worried less about what would happen if I made myself more vulnerable. After feeling so lost, I decided I didn't have anything left to lose.

Like any self-deprecating perfectionist, I had carried a list in my head of the dumbest things I had ever said over the course of my life. I started writing letters to heal these parts of myself, the memories I had carried with me for so long.

I was four years old the first time I felt stupid for saying the wrong thing. We were visiting my parents' friends after the birth of their baby. The mom was nursing, and my brother, then two years old, asked me what she was doing. I whispered to him that she was, "Feeding the baby from her booby." The nursing mom heard and wailed with laughter. She then repeated it to everyone who came over that afternoon. Shamed, I felt like the stupidest thing to ever walk the earth. I should just stop talking. That was the only way to prevent myself from saying something so humiliating again.

Of course, as I got older, I realized that my mom's friend had just thought what I said to be immensely cute, and that is why she repeated it. But whenever I caught myself saying something stupid, I again felt like that humiliated four-year-old. So, I wrote myself a letter from that woman.

I wrote a letter from the boys who found and shared my diary. I apologized from them and told myself that they didn't actually think that I was the dumbest person in the world. That they were sorry that what they thought was a funny game had upset me so much and for so long.

My biggest fear in coaching was that if I did not give a kid enough chances, I would ruin their confidence and their life. And skating parents, gotta love them, had often told me exactly this. But in truth, I regularly gave skaters far too many chances, to the detriment of the team. Aware of this, I became more confident in my coaching and started making braver decisions. A skating mom came after me immediately. Upset, she thought I should have given her daughter more chances to skate in competitions. Truthfully, I should not have placed her daughter on that team level to begin with. I had repeated my old mistake of placing athletes based on potential rather than on track record. I had apologized for that. The mom was still very angry, and it gnawed at me. So, I wrote a letter to myself from her, with expanded perspective, letting me know that she reacted because her daughter was upset. She knew that I wasn't actually trying to crush the souls of children.

I wrote a letter from a coworker who I felt showed me no respect or consideration.

I wrote letters from other colleagues, thanking me for supporting them.

I wrote letters to me from Manny, saying all the things I wished he would say.

I wrote letters from my boys, forgiving me for losing my temper.

Every single day, more letters. Every single day, more love.

NO ONE WILL CHANGE FOR YOU IF YOU'RE NOT WILLING TO CHANGE FOR YOURSELF.

Make it your own. Color, write, or draw and share with our community!

@ashleighrenard | #KeepingItHot

Instructions: Take a break and ask yourself, would you rather:

Get it on in a tent in your backyard?

Spend the night at a swanky hotel?

THIS OR THAT?

What made you choose your answer?

_____

_____

_____

_____

_____

_____

_____

_____

_____

_____

_____

_____

_____

_____

_____

_____

_____

_____

_____

_____

_____

_____

_____

_____

_____

_____

Make a connection. Take a picture and share with a loved one!

What do they think? Start a conversation.

What if you could feel more loved, more appreciated, more cherished — today? What if all this could happen without one single other human changing a thing? That's what Love Letters to Yourself can do.

Instructions: Identify a couple people who you wish would treat you differently. Write yourself a letter from them, saying all the things you'd love for them to say.

Common people to write from include a romantic partner, friend, parent, sibling, child, teacher, boss, or pain in the ass co-worker. The exercise is not about absolving the other person from responsibility. It's about helping you untangle the dynamic you share. When you feel certain about what you deserve, you will have more confidence in asking for your needs to be met, and when setting boundaries.

LOVE LETTERS TO YOURSELF

Person	Wants

Sincerely,

Sincerely,

Sincerely,

Sincerely,

Sincerely,

When my kids are really fighting with each other (beyond the requisite amount of sibling torture), I will send them to their rooms to write a love letter to themselves...from our dog. They can each access, in an instant, what the dog loves about them. Once they find some compassion and tenderness for themselves, they are less likely to look for a fight with their siblings.

Instructions: Write yourself a short love letter from your favorite animal.

FROM YOUR FAVORITE ANIMAL

Sincerely,

Are there people from your past who you wish would have acted differently?

Instructions: Take it to the next level. Revisit and retool the situation by writing a letter from them to you, apologizing, clarifying, and loosening up a bit of the shame and hurt that surrounds the situation.

Person	Situation

FROM THE PAST

Sincerely,

Sincerely,

Sincerely,

Sincerely,

Sincerely,

PART FOUR

ICEBERG, REVISITED

Instructions: Color in each supporting statement below the iceberg to show the fullness you currently feel.

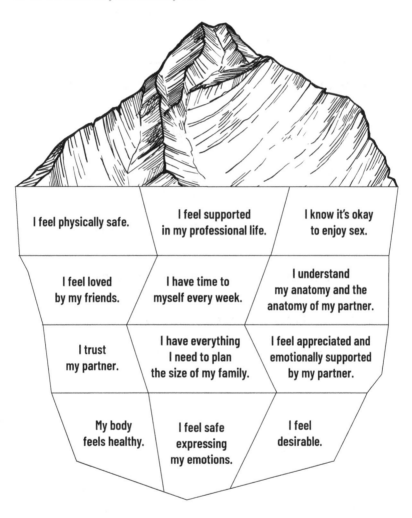

I feel physically safe.

I feel supported in my professional life.

I know it's okay to enjoy sex.

I feel loved by my friends.

I have time to myself every week.

I understand my anatomy and the anatomy of my partner.

I trust my partner.

I have everything I need to plan the size of my family.

I feel appreciated and emotionally supported by my partner.

My body feels healthy.

I feel safe expressing my emotions.

I feel desirable.

MIXING IT UP

Weekday
Sunday Funday (bring out the toys)
Massage Monday (full body massage, with or without sex)
Taco Tuesday (oral only)
Wacky Wednesday (up is down and down is up; make everything different)
Thorough Thursday (full-body treatment)
Foreplay Friday (everything but intercourse)
Sexy Date Night Saturday (once a month, try to get rid of the kids and plan a night where you do it more than once)

FROM *SWING*

On the drive down to the club we were jittery, equal parts eager and skeptical. We found parking, and then set off on foot in the direction of the address that had been emailed to us. As we passed people on the street, I felt nervous. Would they know where we were going? Would they wonder why I was wearing a trench coat? Did I look like a flasher? At last, we saw the fake sign the email had told us to look for: *Señor Rattler's Cantina.* We paused, looked up, and each took a deep breath. "Okay, let's do this," Manny said.

We stepped inside the building we had looked at online for months. It looked just like the pictures, except now it was packed with people.

Heads turned as we walked in, and everyone gave us matching, welcoming smiles. We checked in at the front desk, handing them our confirmation email and IDs so they could check our membership status. Right on cue, a male host magically appeared to greet us as we surrendered our coats and cell phones at coat check.

"Welcome," he said, beaming as he offered his hand. "I'm Chuck. Follow me."

As he led us through the throng of people on the main floor, I noticed that everyone was smiling. The crowd parted for us. Everyone acknowledged us as we walked by, raising their glass, nodding, or giving a little wave. The cheeriness made me feel like we were walking the iconic path in the opening credits for Sesame Street. *Suuuunny day, sweeping the clouuuds awaaay...Coooome and play everything's aaaaa-okaay.*

We unavoidably carried the mark of newcomers. Not only were we being led through the club, but we were wide-eyed, blinking, exhibiting the curiosity of newborn deer. And, my goodness, we must have looked young. Manny, with his Mediterranean bloodline, could grow a five o'clock shadow by 10:00 a.m., but he was still just a couple years away from his college football prime. I was still getting carded in bars. Our rookie status could not have been clearer if a neon sign hung above our heads flashing "Fresh Meat." Despite this, or maybe because of it, the welcome we received felt authentic. It did not feel like the creepy, predatory type of attention I sometimes experienced while out in the world as a woman. From a mile away, these club-goers could tell we were first-timers, and they wanted to assure us of the same thing they wanted to be assured of on their first visit.

Hi! Welcome! We are so glad you are here. No need to be nervous. We are all just normal people.

And they seemed to be. On the outside, they were all remarkably normal-looking people, like you'd encounter at the grocery store. As our host gave us a tour, I tried to guess everyone's occupations. Tattoo artist and hair stylist. Librarian and accountant (or something equally serious).

Chuck led us through the main floor, flanked on one side by a long bar, and opening up on the other side into a restaurant with a buffet. Manny and I had already discussed that seeing someone grab a plate of food was the grossest thing we could imagine witnessing at a sex club.

We squeezed through a mob of people to make our way to the staircase at the back. It twisted up to a landing and to the second floor. Through the low lighting we saw a sea of mattresses, outfitted in sheets of dark purple and blue. Uniform walking paths were visible between the row of mattresses and punctuated by towers of clean dark sheets and white towels throughout.

"This is *the pit*," said Chuck. Following him, we continued our journey up another flight of stairs. The third floor held another bar, a dance floor, locker rooms and showers, and a platform with a dancing pole. Above the platform hung metal hooks anchored into the ceiling. I didn't wonder for long what they would be used for, as a dominatrix set up shop for the evening and a line began to form for her spanking services. Chuck wrapped up his tour, showing us the changing rooms, lockers, and showers. After he bid us adieu, we went back to the third-floor bar for a glass of wine.

"Cheers?" I asked, amused and still hesitant to believe this was all real. I raised my glass to Manny.

"Cheers," he agreed, and we each took a sip as we looked around. We had purposefully arrived late, after 11:00 p.m., and as we took another walk around the third floor, we saw that the club had filled considerably since we arrived. I saw a banister framing a large open area and ushered Manny over to see what was there. As we got closer, we realized it looked down onto what Chuck had referred to as *the pit*.

"Don't worry," said a voice from behind, "that will be packed later in the night." We turned to see a smiling, earnest blonde couple behind us. He was tall and broad-shouldered, with hair cut short. She was petite with a sleek bob.

"I'm Morgan," she said, extending her hand first to me, then to Manny.

"And I'm Tony," he said, extending his hand first to Manny, then to me.

"You guys new here?" asked Morgan.

"Yup, first time," I said, trying to stay cool talking to a real-life swinger. "What about you guys?"

"We usually come once a month," said Morgan, "for a couple years, right, babe?" she looked to Tony for confirmation.

"Yeah, we've been coming for right around two years," he agreed. "But we are starting a new production and won't be back again for a while. That's why we are here tonight: a last hurrah before all our energy goes into our show."

"Show? What kind of show?" I asked and took another sip of my wine. They explained that they were actors, had first met when they were cast in the same play, and they were starting a new stage production that would take every waking minute of their time for the next six months. As we chatted, I noticed the music was lower than at a regular club, which made conversation much easier. We decided to take our conversation to the dance floor. The DJ was just starting a game where three women were blindfolded. They used their hands and their mouths to identify their partner on the dance floor. I thought this was a spectacular idea. I excused us to get another drink. As I leaned over the bar to ask for a glass of wine, Manny pressed himself against me. He wrapped his arms around my waist and spoke into my hair, "I'm horny."

I turned to him and replied through a kiss and a smile, "Me, too."

We took our wine and walked hand-in-hand around the bar. Looking over the banister, the mattresses were indeed filling up. The lights were low throughout the club, but we could see darkened bodies positioning themselves beside and on top of each other, mouths and hands beginning their search. Behind us, along two walls of the third floor, was a wide, L-shaped bench that served as a giant sectional. We turned and leaned our backs against the banister, surveying the party-goers perched along the bench. In front of us sat a man with a woman sitting sideways on his lap. She leaned back to kiss him, and he slid his hand high up the front of her skirt, deep between her thighs. To their left was a foursome, two men and two women. The women were kneeling on the bench and kissing each other as their partners flanked them, sipping on their drinks. We watched as the women stood and began to peel off each other's clothes. They returned to the bench, the men shifting outwards to make more room, and positioned themselves for 69, one woman lying flat on her back and the other snugly on top of her, each cupping her friend's buttocks and burying her face in her crotch.

I felt blood rush quickly between my legs, immediately causing a sensation of fullness and wetness. I decided that I'd had enough watching. "Let's go sit there," I said, motioning toward the corner. We walked hand in hand to my chosen location. I grabbed a towel for Manny to sit on, with his back to the corner. I climbed on to sit facing him, straddling his legs with mine. My back was arched, and when Manny reached around and his hands touched my butt cheeks instead of my skirt, my suspicion was confirmed. My ass was visible to the whole club. As I kissed him firmly, he squeezed and ran his hands up my back, flipping my skirt up completely. I kissed him harder. Out of the corner of my eye I saw Tony and Morgan sit down to our left. They motioned for us to join them. I shook my head and mouthed a "no, thanks" and they replied with "no problem." I felt Manny hard between my legs, and I rubbed against him as we kissed. He ran his lips down my neck and to my right I saw the 69'ing women had reconfigured with their partners and now the men were in on the action, each one of them going down on one of the women. With Manny's face in my boobs, I whispered to him, "I'm going down on you." I slid off him and between his legs. I knelt, white stockings on the floor, and undid his belt and pants. He propped himself up slightly so I could move them down low enough to access his penis. I swirled my tongue around the tip and looked up at him as I took it in my mouth. He looked down at me and scanned the room. As I slid my mouth up and down on his shaft, I gave him a sly smile. I knew the visual and physical stimulation was enough to make him nearly lose his mind.

"Get on top of me," he offered. I giggled as I stood up, dizzy from the excitement. I turned around, reached behind me and pulled my thong to the side. Manny licked his fingers and reached around the front to put them inside me. I leaned into him, laying my back against his chest. He fingered me as he kissed my neck, and I looked out at the dance floor. On the spanking platform, a woman fingered herself as her handcuffed husband was flogged by the masked dominatrix. Beside us, the foursome was now having sex from behind as the women kissed and fondled each other's breasts. Tony was fingering Morgan and licking her clit, and she looked like she was about to climax. And then I realized so was I.

"I'm close," I whispered. Upon hearing this, Manny steadied the rhythm of his palm over my clitoris, keeping his fingers inside me. I closed my eyes, needing to focus on the building heat and intensity in my body and block out everything in my gaze. My body clenched, every muscle tight, as my orgasm exploded like a volcano, sending torrid streaks up my chest and over my ears. I stretched back, my cheek against Manny's and told him I was coming. Eyes pressed shut, I saw a rainbow explosion, a kaleidoscope of color that kept spinning behind my eyelids. I fell limp on top of him and looked toward the ceiling. My vision was foggy, but I felt Manny's body beneath me and the bass from the music rattle through the bench under our bodies. Finally, I let my eyes drift down and my vision quickly sharpened. The sex scenes around us seemed to have doubled. Everywhere I looked I saw different configurations of mouth and flesh.

I turned my eyes to Manny's. "I want you inside me, now," I insisted. I put my fingers in my mouth, scooping saliva to stroke down his penis. I positioned myself and took him inside me, lowering until my glutes pressed against him, spreading to his hip bones. He grasped my waist, fingers on my abdomen and each thumb lateral of my spine, allowing me to feel the contraction of my back extensors under his thumbs as I arched back and forth on top of him. I rose to my toes and pressed my hands on my knees, my arms pressing my breasts together as I rode him, all the while continuing to watch the scene in front of me unfold.

I hope after reading one of my favorite sex scenes from *Swing* you are feeling inspired.

Instructions: Get your creative juices (and ahem, maybe some other juices) flowing and write a sexy story, for your eyes only.

SEX SCENE

Instructions: Now that your creative juices are flowing a bit more, draw a scene from your sexy story.

IT IS MY FANTASY TO:

Make a connection. Take a picture and share with a loved one!

What do they think? Start a conversation.

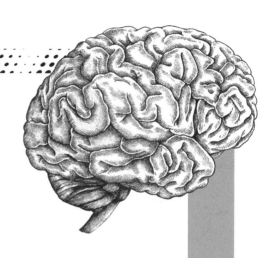

WHAT'S ON YOUR MIND?

Instructions: Take a break and ask yourself, would you rather:

Get twelve hugs a day from your partner?

Have twelve things put away in the house?

THIS OR THAT?

What made you choose your answer?

Make a connection. Take a picture and share with a loved one!

What do they think? Start a conversation.

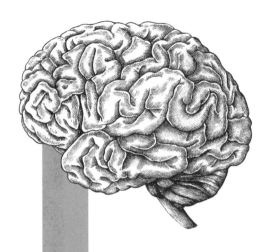

WHAT'S ON YOUR MIND?

PART FIVE

THERE'S A REASON WHY THEY ALWAYS SUSPECT THE SPOUSE.

Make it your own. Color, write, or draw and share with our community!

@ashleighrenard | #KeepingItHot

AIRING GRIEVANCES

Constructive criticism is not easy for me to hear. I aim to be perfect, always — can't you tell I'm trying? But, if I want to stay married, I've got to listen.

Early on, Manny and I established a protocol for airing grievances, and it stuck. When one of us is annoyed with something completely annoying that the other annoying person annoyingly did or forgot or did wrong (how annoying), we start the conversation with, "Is the Complaint Department open?" The other person then can say yes or no. If they say no, then we hold the complaint for another time, but it's almost always a yes.

It's funny, and weird. But it also works.

Here's why. You may think (well, I thought for a long time) that it works because the person accepting the grievance can say yes or no.

But I recently realized that the real reason is that it shifts the energy into a space where the criticism can be constructive because the grievance holder (a.k.a. the person who is annoyed that their partner is so damn annoying) has to take a beat, and a breath, and approach the other in a manner consistent with the rules of the Complaint Department.

There is no storming across the house. There is no shouting from another room. There is no snarky text. We duck our head into the room where the other person is resting their annoying ass and ask officially and cordially, like we would if we were inquiring at a hotel restaurant if the breakfast buffet was still open.

No? Okay, I'll figure something else out. And we do.

But 90% of the time the Complaint Department is open. The annoying person listens to the annoyed and says something like, "Got it," or "Received."

If the annoying person is surprised by the complaint they may say, "Really? That's surprising."

The annoyed person will respond with, "Really."

The annoying person then says something like, "Got it," or "Received."

And what happens when a previously issued complaint comes up again? The Complaint Department protocol does not differ. We do not add the words we're thinking, which may or may not go something like this: *OMFG I cannot believe they did it again, that dumb-as-shit MFer, FUUUUUCK.*

Instead, the annoyed person will duck their head in and neutrally say, "Babe, is the Complaint Department open?"

Annoying person will say yes if they know what's good for them.

Annoyed person will recite the complaint.

Annoying person will pause for half a second, trying to register whether they just felt a mini earthquake or if there was a glitch in the matrix, because this feels like déjà vu, and say, "Ahh...this is a repeater, isn't it? Dammit, I thought I was going to remember that one. Sorry, babe. Got it. Received."

Need more room? Get half-price digital worksheets here.

COMPLAINT DEPARTMENT

Instructions: Use this as a space to record your issued complaints to reflect on in the future.

Date:
Grievance Issued:

Resolution:

Date:
Grievance Issued:

Resolution:

Date:
Grievance Issued:

Resolution:

Date:
Grievance Issued:

Resolution:

GRIEVANCE ISSUED

COMPLAINT DEPARTMENT

Instructions: Use this as a space to record your received complaints to reflect on in the future.

Date:
Grievance Received:

Resolution:

Date:
Grievance Received:

Resolution:

Date:
Grievance Received:

Resolution:

Date:
Grievance Received:

Resolution:

GRIEVANCE RECEIVED

You had $5k to go on a sexy trip for two?

Your had $5k to renovate your bedroom?

THIS OR THAT?

What made you choose your answer?

Make a connection. Take a picture and share with a loved one!

What do they think? Start a conversation.

FROM *SWING*

After my boys were done nursing, I always put them to bed the same way: I cuddled them and whispered to them a list of all the people who loved them. "Mommy loves you. And Daddy loves you. And Yiayia loves you. And Papou loves you. And Grandma loves you. And Grandpa loves you..." I would go through all our family members, our friends, and our pets. I repeated it over and over until they fell asleep, or I did.

Jack and Luke always lay silently, just listening. But Niko enjoyed the list so much that he often responded with enthusiasm, "Oh, yes. I *know* they love me."

He was certain, so perfectly certain. And I loved that he was certain. And I also wondered what it would feel like to feel that certain that I was loved. No matter how often I brought up my desire for us to be more connected, Manny fell back into his old habits of being disconnected from me and the boys. I knew that I wanted better for our family. I wondered if the next thing on my list of things to do that I judged other women for doing was to leave my husband.

"Babe," I said to him one night.

"Uh, yeah." He looked up from the kitchen sink.

"I want you to know I am not mad," I started, "and things aren't really bad..."

He tilted his head like a perplexed puppy.

"But I wonder if we should really stay together. I want the boys to have more than we have, and I am getting tired of wanting that from you if you don't want it, too."

I told him that I was still unhappy in our marriage. If I left him now, it would be for the boys, not despite them. I wanted a family that demonstrated love and connection. I was determined to show them that affection and appreciation were not things only girls and women offered or needed. Our sons deserved more love and affection from him, but he also deserved to feel how good it felt to offer it. It was essential for our boys and the people they would love in the future that they were comfortable expressing their emotions. I did not want to be the only parent to model this. And even if I never found a partner who could show them, at least they would remember that I wanted to set the bar higher for them and for their future relationships. I wanted them to always be certain they were loved.

I didn't yell. I didn't cry. I didn't stomp my foot. I told him calmly.

And he heard me. I think for the first time.

I don't know if it was my certainty, my resolve, or the fact that I had grown myself into a new version of me, but after a lifetime of being trained to ignore the sound of a woman's voice, he finally heard me. I had been unmuted.

"Babe," he said, looking at me through tears, "all I want is to be with you and the boys, forever." He wiped his cheeks. "I'll do anything."

Manny and I had never fallen head over heels in love with each other, but at some point, we had both fallen madly in love with the family we had grown. Finally, the fear of being vulnerable had become less scary than the fear of losing his family. He agreed he wanted to make things better than ever. He even agreed to start seeing [my therapist].

I resisted the urge to ask much about their sessions, but he did volunteer one of her assignments. He was to begin giving me twelve hugs a day. I also hoped that Jacki was in the process of giving him an energy extreme makeover, an affection boot camp, a list of 72 things a day he should do to help him open up emotionally. I hoped there were plans to balance his chakras, cleanse his aura, and reflect on past lives. I hadn't even done all these things, but I was certain he would require them. But I didn't ask about any other details, and we focused on a family hug project, ensuring each of our boys each got twelve hugs a day, too.

The hugs often stretched out, turning into chats or cuddles. The boys began to use the hugs as an opportunity to ask us questions or tell us how they were doing. These small acts of affection became our touchstones, our guaranteed times of connection, even on the busiest or most stressful of days. Almost immediately, the boys seemed happier. They were more affectionate, and their manners improved.

I began to understand the intent behind the assignment. Romantic, demonstrative love was something that Manny and I had subconsciously struck from our agreement at the very beginning. Affection was for children, and in the Greek custom, only to be offered by women. We didn't need that. We were already confident enough, grown-up enough. We had love. We had love like people have an antique vase, up high on a shelf. Or like a couple would check their apartment for appliances before making a wedding registry. Yes, we had that already. Check that box.

But somewhere along the line I had decided I wanted more. I wanted to *feel* love. I wanted love to swirl through our house, to wrap around each one of us, to give us a feeling of warmth and buoyancy, to be more alive and electric than was possible for an old vase on a high shelf. I didn't want love, the noun. I wanted love, the verb. It was love the verb that I felt when cuddling Niko to sleep, when he told me he was certain that all those people loved him. Love was not a box he had checked. It was assurance in action, in the way faces lit up when he walked into the room. The way people glowed back at him, mirroring his light when they were with him.

Day by day, hug by hug, love stopped being something we *had*. It became something we *did*. We became people who were tended to.

I thought about the difference between the work of gardening and the tending of gardening. The work was strenuous. It was tiring and sometimes mindless. It could be hired out. It was essentially the checking of boxes. *Raised beds built?* Check. *Compost ordered and delivered?* Check. *Seeds planted?* Check.

Tending a garden was different. It involved the gentle guiding of a vine over a trellis. It required watching the forecast and carefully planning when to water. It called for attention, protection, concern. It took multiple visits to the plant to see if our actions were helping it thrive. In the tending, we saw our care mirrored back to us. Work can build a garden, but tending makes it grow.

Manny and I had both signed on to do the work of building our life together, but we hadn't known about the tending. We liked checking boxes. We liked moving along in life like it was a road, one signpost after another, showing us that we were making progress, proving to the people around us that they needn't worry about us because we were on the right track.

But it's not a road. It was never a road.

It's a garden.

Need more room? Get half-price digital worksheets here.

Instructions: Take a break and ask yourself, would you rather:

Get it on in a hot tub?

Get it on in a sauna?

THIS OR THAT?

What made you choose your answer?

Make a connection. Take a picture and share with a loved one!

What do they think? Start a conversation.

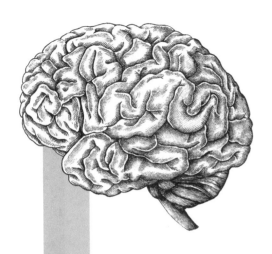

WHAT'S ON YOUR MIND?

PART SIX

WELCOME TO EARTH SCHOOL

Assignment: babysit this meat suit

Term: a few minutes - 120 years

Review from past visitor: ☆☆☆☆☆

Super complicated most of the time, but the dogs and coffee are incredible!

At first, I thought the brain was going to make this experience awesome and so easy, but then I realized most of my time was spent getting myself out of situations my brain got me into. So now I try to listen to my gut. And yes, that's the part that's also responsible for pooping. Earth School is a trip!

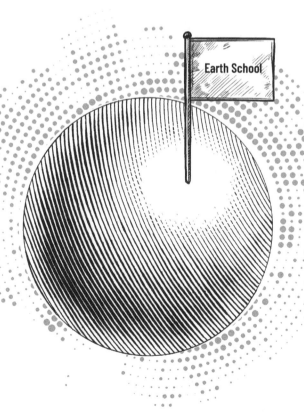

INSTRUCTIONS FOR CARING FOR YOUR MEAT SUIT — IF IT HATES EVERYONE: FEED IT. IF IT THINKS EVERYONE HATES IT: PUT IT TO SLEEP.

Make it your own. Color, write, or draw and share with our community!

@ashleighrenard | #KeepingItHot

MEAT SUIT NAVIGATORS

Instructions: Please declare your preferences for your stay here at Earth School.

Movement: How would you like to move this meat suit?

_____

_____

_____

_____

_____

_____

_____

Pleasure: How would you like to enjoy this meat suit?

_____

_____

_____

_____

_____

_____

Nutrition: How would you like to fuel this meat suit?

_____

_____

_____

_____

_____

_____

PREFERENCES

Communication: How would you like to talk to this meat suit and its big, beautiful human brain, which seems really smart but spins stories and fuels anxieties and asks dumb questions like, "Does anyone really like me?"

_____

_____

_____

_____

_____

_____

_____

_____

_____

_____

_____

_____

_____

_____

_____

_____

_____

_____

_____

_____

_____

_____

_____

_____

_____

_____

LIFE DOESN'T HAVE TO BE PERFECT TO BE WONDERFUL.

Make it your own. Color, write, or draw and share with our community!

Instructions: Take a break and ask yourself, would you rather:

Have a strap on used on you?

Use one on your partner?

THIS OR THAT?

What made you choose your answer?

_____

_____

_____

_____

_____

_____

_____

_____

_____

_____

_____

_____

_____

_____

_____

_____

_____

_____

_____

_____

_____

_____

_____

Make a connection. Take a picture and share with a loved one!

What do they think? Start a conversation.

FROM *SWING*

My pregnancies were easy, but my labors were long, eighty hours total for the three. During each contraction I looked deep into the discomfort, like an explorer, diving, drilling deeper into the core of the pain with a curious mind. Every intense training session I had ever done as an athlete was a perfect preparation for labor. Over and over, I had shown myself that I could tolerate any measure of physical pain if I knew it was bringing me closer to a goal. I knew the key was to let go of resistance, to not spend the whole time condemning the pain. In between contractions I was vomiting and looking the opposite of Zen, but during every contraction I would relax my body and go deeper. I could manage this until the very end with Jack and Luke, then I would tense up, unable to handle the intensity of transition before pushing.

But when I was in labor with Niko, I was finally able to lie still and completely relax during the hardest portion of labor. Manny lay in bed beside me, sleeping, as I lay silent and still for each contraction. It was in these last hours of my final birth that I realized for the first time that each contraction started at the top of my uterus and worked its way down. During every contraction, I lay limp as I had the sensation that the top of my head was opening, and the entire Universe was ripping through my body. And then it would stop. And I would touch my body with amazement, that I was in one piece and still alive. It was in that moment that I realized we can handle excruciating pain, pain we are certain will kill us, and come out whole.

The key was not trying to rush it. The key was not to resist. To not diagnose the reason and the meaning and then push the feeling aside. If things were moving more slowly than I would like, I needed to trust that it was because there was more for me to learn. More information for me to seek out and bring back.

I knew curiosity could save me when it felt like pain and impatience were trying to slaughter me. Curiosity could turn my pain into purpose.

CURIOSITY TRANSFORMS MY PAIN INTO PURPOSE.

Make it your own. Color, write, or draw and share with our community!

Instructions: Take a break and ask yourself, would you rather:

☐

Surprise your partner with oral when they are working on their computer?

☐

Have your partner surprise you with oral while you are working?

THIS OR THAT?

What made you choose your answer?

Make a connection. Take a picture and share with a loved one!

What do they think? Start a conversation.

Instructions: Consider something that is really freaking hard right now. Write about it.

_____
_____
_____
_____
_____
_____
_____
_____
_____
_____
_____
_____
_____
_____
_____
_____
_____
_____
_____
_____
_____
_____
_____
_____
_____

HARDSHIPS

Instructions: Consider the lessons or opportunities that may be here for you within this struggle. This is not about spiritual bypass or self-gaslighting. This thing sucks. It hurts. You want it to change. But what lesson have you learned despite the overall shittiness of the experience? Did any realizations come about that would have been hard to see otherwise? Is there any part you are grateful for? Write about it.

Instructions: Grab markers or colored pencils in three colors: green, yellow, and red.

Color in the clock with your stress level at different times of the day.

CLOCK EXERCISE

MONDAY TO FRIDAY

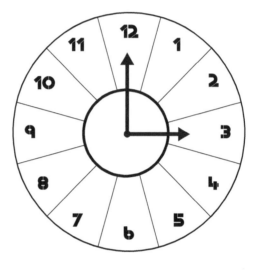

SATURDAY AND SUNDAY

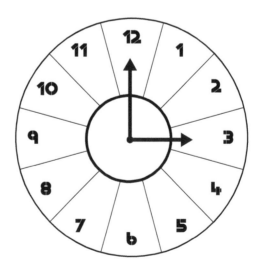

Instructions: Grab markers or colored pencils in three colors: green, yellow, and red.

Color in the clock with your stress level at different times of the day for schedules outside of your average week.

ALTERNATE SCHEDULE ONE

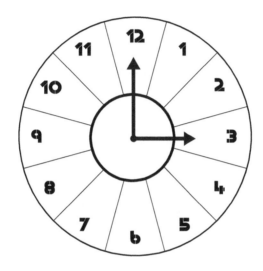

ALTERNATE SCHEDULE TWO

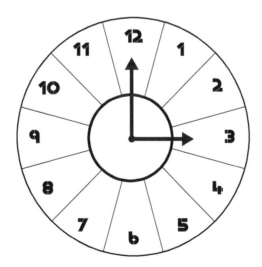

Instructions: Reflect on the previous exercise by answering the following questions.

What times are a struggle in your day?

_____

_____

_____

_____

_____

_____

_____

Is there a difference between weekdays and weekends?

_____

_____

_____

_____

_____

_____

_____

In the red zones, write out all the happenings, using your five senses.

_____

_____

_____

_____

_____

_____

_____

Which part is so predictable?

_____

_____

_____

_____

_____

_____

What can be moved to another time to prevent this conflict?

_____

_____

_____

_____

_____

_____

_____

What routine or ritual can be established to eliminate or reduce the conflict?

_____

_____

_____

_____

_____

_____

_____

Mornings in our house used to go like this: three children rifling through baskets of clean laundry, trying to find something to wear. It resulted in wrinkled clothes all over the floor, covered in dog hair, plus kids worried they would be late and sibling accusations of garment stealing. Who am I to interrupt a good time? But now we dump all the baskets of clean laundry on the bed after dinner and work together to get it put away. Within ten minutes we have the bed cleared off and every clean item of clothing is in its proper place. Mornings may bring their own stressors, but they are not laundry-related.

Family rule: When we are doing a job together, we are not all done until the job is all done.

Need more room? Get half-price digital worksheets here.

INTIMACY POST-PARTUM EXPERT WEIGH IN FROM LC De SHAY, BA, CMlc, IBCLC; PMH-C CANDIDATE

Six weeks: that's how long your medical team will tell you it takes before you are "healed" after giving birth (eight weeks if you had a complicated surgical birth). Extolling the wonders of the human body is one thing, but expecting this superhero level of bounce-back is another.

The space between what we imagine pregnancy, birth, and parenting will be and how it really unfolds is vast. As vast as the distance between meeting the minimum clinical requirements for birth recovery to safely survive a sexual encounter without infection or traumatic injury, versus being emotionally ready and physically eager to have one.

There is no gentle way to put this: the pursuit of intimate fulfillment is for many people an inaccessible privilege.

Being able to pursue and prioritize pleasure requires:

A safe home life, rest, food, and the support of another able-bodied adult — one who loves you enough to help for free or whom you have enough money to employ.

The next monumental barrier to intimacy is — UNEQUAL DISTRIBUTION OF LABOR. Yes, I am yelling. The expectation that the same people recovering from birthing the baby should wash, bathe, cook, clean, fix, cope, comfort, hold, launder, fold, and otherwise do the work of two to four adults is delusional at best and oppressive at worst.

Lose it. Period.

Replace it with the well confirmed knowledge that the partners in new parent relationships who have the most sex with their spouses are those who do the largest share of household duties.

Equity is foreplay.

Communication is the lifeblood of relationships, and as I tell my clients and patients all the time, the lubrication of our sexiest, most romantic organ of all: the mind.

The following exercises in rephrasing will save you a world of hurt, so practice them (and if you think it might help, get a therapist to help you understand why you need to rephrase them this way):

Instead of	Try
"So what did you do all day today?"	**"What is it like being here for hours with the baby?"**
Follow-up questions: What could be done before I leave, or while I am gone to make things easier/more efficient/less stressful?	
"Must be nice being able to go to work."	**"How do you feel being responsible for the household salary right now?"**
Follow-up questions: Do you ever wish you were home with the baby instead? Why or why not? How can we create more balance for you to do caregiving and for me to do independent activities for myself and the household?	
"It's like we are never going to have sex again."	**"What do you miss about the time we used to spend together, before the baby was born?"**
Follow-up questions: Is there anything we can do to create the same (fill in the blank feelings/experiences) so that we can have fun together now that the baby is here? What are some activities that you would enjoy doing as a family? As a couple? By yourself? Let's see what creative ways we can come up with to accomplish this.	
"Nobody prepared us for this/it's a trick."	**"What has surprised you the most/ least since the birth of the baby?"**
Follow-up: Do you feel comfortable telling me your fears about these changes? What things can we do to reduce our anxiety about change, and how would you like to tackle it together?	

Reframing is a powerful tool. It doesn't replace the necessary vulnerability to tell the absolute truth about our experiences, but it does take that truth and make it the fertilizer from which we can make the most of the world we're in, rather than merely sitting stuck in the frustration of how things may have been. Take these concepts and use them during hard conversations to find a way to create interactions you can enjoy, however humble they may be.

In *Come As You Are*, Emily Nagowski clarifies the difference between "spontaneous" versus "responsive" desire. Precious little is spontaneous in any sense of the word after you have kids (besides your baby's insistence on needing to eat every time you take a shower), but one thing that is LEAST likely to be spontaneous is sexual arousal.

So how can we cultivate or create a space to enjoy physical contact in the life of a person obligated to provide that to a tiny human all day?

First: remove expectations. Resist the impulse to compare what now works or feels good to before, or what has changed physically and perhaps what needs to change environmentally to feel good. Rather than seeking to resume what you had before the baby, spend time talking about what you want to create in your new bodies now that you have the baby.

Secondly: abandon judgment. The reflex to see our own evolving needs and desires as worthy of scorn is deeply entrenched in so many of us. A mantra to repeat and meditate on is *change is a sign of life, if you aren't growing, adapting, changing, or evolving in some way, that is nature's warning of decay.* See the changes in what you want, and how you enjoy getting it, as a means of your body and mind progressing to give you pleasure in life.

Last: quality over quantity. A huge foundation for desire is wanting, and we generally do not want things we constantly have in the palm of our hands. As such, judging a relationship of new parents by the number of times they have sensual contact, as opposed to how titillating and mutually satisfying it is when they do, is missing the point. Nothing builds up desire like anticipation, so rather than forcing the issue to meet some imaginary quota, spend time planning for and fantasizing about how you can make the most of the time you do have, when you have it.

LC De Shay, BA, CMlc, IBCLC; PMH-C Candidate (she/they) is a professional in reproductive psychosociology. In the last 15 years she dedicated her time to research in high risk, maternal-child health, and parent support, working in clinics, hospitals, universities and research programs. She now concentrates her work on intersectional needs of femmes (women + gender expansive) in high stress circumstances, where she believes intimacy fulfillment is central to mental and public health, using humanist expansion of technology to do so.

LC is a remarried mother of 4, a DV survivor, and an avid disability adaptation advocate; she splits her time between Europe and California, crocheting, gardening, and loving all things Blerd (Black Nerds!).

Need more room? Get half-price digital worksheets here.

GROWN-UPS ONLY

Instructions: Choose three jobs to swap with your partner for one week.

Yourself	Partner
Chore: Additional Notes:	Chore: Additional Notes:
Chore: Additional Notes:	Chore: Additional Notes:
Chore: Additional Notes:	Chore: Additional Notes:

Do you have any worries about your partner's ability to do the job?

_____

_____

_____

Your ability to do the job?

_____

_____

_____

SOFT SWAP

Did any feelings come up when you saw how your partner completed the job?

Will you stick with this switch or do the jobs differently moving forward?

NOTHING MAKES ME PROUDER THAN CHILD LABOR.

Make it your own. Color, write, or draw and share with our community!

I HATE IT ALL:
HOW TO FIGURE OUT WHAT JOBS
YOUR KIDS LIKE

When I call the kids to come tidy, they come quickly, because whoever gets there first gets to pick their job. Here's the child labor ninja trick: I have a different list in my head depending on who comes first. I know which chores they each find least offensive based on their personalities (more on that in a bit), so I make sure I always include the favorite chore of the child who comes first.

Not only do they get to choose, but they always get their favorite.

It's magic, I tell you.

Here's an adaptation for only children: If they come quickly, they have five jobs to choose from, then three, then two. If they dilly dally, then there is no choice.

HOW TO CHOOSE CHORES FOR YOUR KIDS BASED ON THEIR PERSONALITIES

For Efficiency Experts

I won't say Jack is lazy, but damn is he efficient. Someday he'll make millions teaching companies how to save money by cutting corners and still getting the job done, but for now he drives me bonkers with his assessment of when a chore is "done." The hack that has saved our relationship and my sanity is choosing jobs for him very carefully. I have him do jobs that have a simple done/not done assessment, like emptying the garbage cans, refilling things, unpacking deliveries, or putting away groceries.

For Perfectionists

Where Jack avoids details and careful execution, Luke obsesses, so much so that doing a job with sloppy siblings irritates him considerably. I let him do jobs that need a high degree of accuracy, like folding kitchen linens (it's not surgery, but the napkins and kitchen towels only fit if they are folded a certain way) or carefully putting away Christmas decorations. I also let him work alone most of the time. Collaborative jobs stress him out. He plays sports and has lots of friends; I am not raising an anti-social kid. But in chores, I let him use his strengths.

For Social Butterflies

Niko just wants to have fun, and guess what, chatting about Pokémon while folding his clothes or doing a job alongside me is super fun for him. He also has great stamina to help me with a long job if we are talking and laughing throughout.

KIDS TOO

Instructions: Choose a job that you never, ever want to do again. Then, either:

- Assign it to another member of the family, then train them on how to execute it (this is my vote).

- Never ever do it again (try this for a bit and see if it actually needs to be done).

- Hire an outside person to do it.

Job	Current Doer	New Action Plan

FULL SWAP

In the future, when you notice this job is not done and should damn well be done, you have three options:

1. Ask the job holder to do it as soon as possible.

2. Ask someone else in the family to do it.

3. Ignore it.

The thing is that this job is now off-limits for you. If there are other humans in your house, you do not need to do everything. We all need to recognize which burdens are not ours to hold.

If you can easily, joyfully, and with no resistance hand off a job that has always been yours to another person, amazing. Move on to the next page and send me your rate for life coaching. If you're like me and have near-panic attacks every time your spouse washes the dishes (like I did for nearly a year after Manny took over that job), here's an exercise for you (okay, us):

Look up "Donna Eden Daily Energy Routine" and "Brad Yates EFT Tapping" both on YouTube.

Need more room? Get half-price digital worksheets here.

Instructions: Draw a floorplan of your house. Grab three colors: green, yellow, and red. Color in the parts of the house with the general feeling of ease or conflict that you experience there, with red being "very conflicted," yellow being "somewhat conflicted," and green being "not at all conflicted."

HOUSE FLOORPLAN

Instructions: Reflect on what parts of your house are hot spots. For these red zones, objectively write out the situations that take place there. Imagine you are watching through a surveillance camera and writing a log of the activities. Who's in the room? When does another person enter? What happens first? Then next?

HOUSE HOT SPOTS

What about this is a surprise?

_____

_____

_____

_____

_____

_____

Which part is so predictable?

_____

_____

_____

_____

_____

_____

What can be moved to another part of the house to prevent this conflict?

_____

_____

_____

_____

_____

_____

What routine or ritual can be established to eliminate the conflict?

_____

_____

_____

_____

_____

Instructions: Draw a floorplan of your workspace. Grab three colors: green, yellow, and red. Color in the parts of the workspace with the general feeling of ease or conflict that you experience there, with red being "very conflicted," yellow being "somewhat conflicted," and green being "not at all conflicted."

WORKSPACE FLOORPLAN

Instructions: Reflect on what parts of your workspace are hot spots. For these red zones, objectively write out the situations that take place there. Imagine you are watching through a surveillance camera and writing a log of the activities. Who's in the room? When does another person enter? What happens first? Then next?

WORKSPACE HOT SPOTS

What about this is a surprise?

Which part is so predictable?

What can be moved to another part of the workspace to prevent this conflict?

What routine or ritual can be established to eliminate the conflict?

Instructions: Take a break and ask yourself, would you rather:

Try to set a record for orgasms in one day?

See how many days in a row you can be intimate?

THIS OR THAT?

What made you choose your answer?

_____

_____

_____

_____

_____

_____

_____

_____

_____

_____

_____

_____

_____

_____

_____

_____

_____

_____

_____

_____

_____

_____

_____

Make a connection. Take a picture and share with a loved one!

What do they think? Start a conversation.

FLIP THE RINK

In my years of coaching, when repetition and correction couldn't correct an error, I had a trick I would pull out of my sleeve. I would flip the rink.

See, when a team performs, they always know which side is "judges' side," where the officials will be sitting during a competition. Because competition facilities and locker room layout determine which door a team will use to enter the ice, judges' side is the constant to determine where the team will set up for the program.

When an element was being performed incorrectly, I'd try all my usual tricks: verbal correction, demonstration, on-ice video review. When nothing seemed to change, I'd call out, "FLIP THE RINK," and the team would set up to perform the program or element with their orientation flipped.

Do you know what happened every single time?

I wish I could say the program became perfect and we all took the rest of the day off and enjoyed limitless hot chocolate at the snack bar, but not quite. The element didn't become perfect, but the execution always changed. And I don't know about you, but I'd rather work on a new problem than an old one.

HOW CAN YOU FLIP THE RINK IN YOUR OWN HOME?

Fighting in the kitchen during breakfast? Try eating breakfast in the living room for a week.

Sibling arguments? Pushing and shoving in the bathroom in the morning? Grab a water glass and put the toothbrushes in a cupboard in the kitchen.

Instructions: Reflect on activities in your house or workspace that have the most conflict. Where do they occur? Describe the conflict. Come up with a different location in your house or workspace where these activities could be done.

Current Location:
Conflict:

Flipped Location:

Current Location:
Conflict:

Flipped Location:

Current Location:
Conflict:

Flipped Location:

Current Location:
Conflict:

Flipped Location:

FLIPPING LOCATIONS

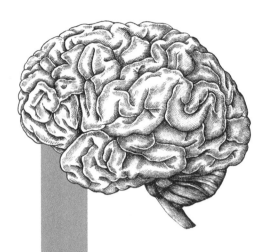

WHAT'S ON YOUR MIND?

PART SEVEN

"Like most moms out there, since having kids my libido dropped. My brain was and is always preoccupied, so I find it hard to just wind down and be present in the moment of sex. Not sure how it came to be, but our thing that has helped spice things up and loosened me up is weed. A part of me has wondered, Is it bad that I rely on this to enjoy sex? I asked my husband this as well, and his response was, 'Who cares?! It works for us, and we like it!' So usually on a Friday and/or a Saturday after the kids have gone to sleep, we enjoy smoking a joint together. We both relax and have good conversation, sometimes about things we would never normally talk about. I have time to myself later with a bath and get cleaned up. He has a shower. We talk beforehand, if we want to use toys, lingerie, etc. and we turn some sexy music on (have made my own bedroom playlist) and get it on. My mind is completely present, and I am so relaxed and enjoy every minute, which of course makes him enjoy every minute as well!"

Jackie (she/her)

EXPERT WEIGH IN FROM DANIELLE SIMONE BRAND, AUTHOR OF *WEED MOM: THE CANNA-CURIOUS WOMAN'S GUIDE TO HEALTHIER RELAXATION, HAPPIER PARENTING, AND CHILLING TF OUT*

"I've had plenty of wonderful orgasms in my life, but never the G-spot kind — until...well, until I smoked a bowl of Sour Diesel, generously applied THC serum to my lady parts, and got down to playtime with my husband. Inhaling the fragrant smoke, my endocannabinoid receptors were massaged and my sense of touch ignited. And the serum's effects were like a sprinkling of fairy dust on my most sensitive parts. You know the Medieval paintings of the saints, or the Virgin Mary, with those glowing, golden orbs encircling cherubic heads upturned in prayer? That was me — only the glowy orb emanated from deep in my center and pulsed itself in unrelenting waves of *hell yeahs* through my entire body. Afterwards, I felt positively weak with pleasure — like a pool of molasses or well-kneaded dough. Virgin indeed."

— from *Weed Mom: The Canna-Curious Woman's Guide to Healthier Relaxation, Happier Parenting, and Chilling TF Out*

As you can tell from the above excerpt, I, a 43-year-old mother of two, think sex and cannabis are a fantastic combo. And I'm not alone. A 2017 Stanford University study found that cannabis users have more sex than non-users — 20% more, in fact[1] — while in another study, 68.5% of women who got down while high described sex as more pleasurable, 60.6% said weed boosted their sex drive, and 52.8% found their orgasms more powerful.[2]

The research makes a lot of sense, given that endocannabinoids (a.k.a. the cannabis-like molecules made by our own bodies) play a role in sexual arousal for women.[3] Given this infromation, we can hypothesize that plant-based cannabinoids such as THC and CBD might also contribute to that sexy feeling. Cannabis lowers stress, relieves pain and anxiety, and acts as a vasodilator, meaning it opens blood vessels and increases blood flow — all good things for enhancing arousal and orgasm. Additionally, cannabis relaxes muscles, heightens sensitivity and sensation, and — in the right dose — can help you be more mentally present. To sum up, cannabis is a helpful tool when it comes to women and sex because it can address the kinds of things — stress, pain, worry, self-consciousness, and feeling disconnected from your body — that tend to get in the way of female pleasure.

Better Communication & Enhanced Partnering

According to several women I interviewed for *Weed Mom*, cannabis can help deepen emotional intimacy and enhance feelings of connection with a partner both in and out of the bedroom. One of the ways it does this is by helping reduce shame and self-censorship so that you can give and receive feedback more openly. In an unguarded state, you may more easily hear your partner's needs and desires and express your own. A study has also found links between cannabinoids and oxytocin, the "hug hormone," showing that THC may boost bonding behavior.[4]

Effects Are Dose-Dependent

This would be a good time to let you know that this suite of amazing sex-and-intimacy-related effects is a largely dose-dependent kind of deal. "Elevate" too much and you may just wanna cuddle up with a pint of Ben & Jerry's and binge a new season of your favorite show, or you may become overactive mentally and lose track of your sensual self. Present in your body, connected with your partner, and consciously elevated — that's the sweet spot for combining cannabis and sex, and to achieve that state, you'll want to dose appropriately. Here's how.

Product and Dosing Recommendations

- Finesse the mood with a CBD-infused massage oil — the non-psychotropic (i.e., it won't get you high), pain-relieving compound combined with loving touch can help provide a fabulous segue to foreplay and more. Brand recommendations: Papa & Barkley, White Fox Nectars, Moon Mother Hemp Co.

- CBD-infused lubes may relieve pain and inflammation, while THC-infused lubes can both relax the vagina and increase blood flow to the area — which in turn heightens sensation and arousal. Brand recommendations: Foria, Kiskanu, Quim. (Each of these makes a CBD-only product as well as a THC-infused one.)

- Inhaling (including smoking, vaping, and vaporizing) is probably the easiest way to consume before sex because of its quick onset. Over time, you can experiment with different strains to find what brings you to the sweetest spots. Remember that sex comes in different moods and flavors; a single strain probably won't meet all your needs. That said, frequently cited THC-dominant strains in the sex and weed convo include: Sour Diesel, Blackjack, Jack Herer, Sherbet, Wedding Cake, Jilly Bean, Do-Si-Dos, and Zkittelez.

- For a midday quickie, try inhaling a high-CBD strain to ease anxiety and help you stay clear-headed enough to get back to work or parenting afterwards. AC/DC is a CBD-rich strain that won't get you high, and Harlequin, another CBD-dominant variety, packs just enough THC to provide a tingle.

- If inhaling isn't your thing but you want to experiment with THC, try a low-dose edible or sublingual. A dose of 2.5-5mg THC is a good place to start. Edibles are associated with delayed onset and a relaxed vibe — aka a "body high" — so take care not to overdo it. Most THC products vary in availability by state, but Wana Brands and Wyld both make reliable edibles that are available in most states with an adult-use THC market.

It'll take some experimentation to find the best products and dose, because your endocannabinoid system is uniquely yours; always "start low and go slow" if you're new to combining weed and sex. It may sound minimal, but a 2.5mg THC edible, or a single puff of a vape or a joint, may provide you with all the sex-positive elevation you need. Says Ashley Manta, a 420-friendly sex educator I interviewed for *Weed Mom*, "You can always add more, but you can't subtract. And if you've gone too far, you're kinda fucked — and not in the fun way."

Weed, Sex, & Men

For male partners, incorporating the right dose of THC may help lessen anxiety, increase focus, and boost blood flow and erections. Too much weed, however, tends to have the opposite effect; when it comes to weed and sex for men, less is probably more.

And if your partner isn't interested, or able, to experiment with cannabis, remember that it's perfectly fine for one person to enjoy herbal relaxation while the other abstains — if both parties are cool with it. Just like in all things couples-related, good communication is key. Keep talking to your partner during your cannabis-enhanced experience, and touch base about it afterward, too. With a little planning and intentionality, cannabis can enhance your sex life in numerous — and utterly delightful — ways.

––––––––––––––––

Danielle Simone Brand (she/her) is a freelance writer and the author of Weed Mom: The Canna-Curious Woman's Guide to Healthier Relaxation, Happier Parenting, and Chilling TF Out *(Ulysses Press, 2020). A few years ago, she wouldn't have self-described as a "weed mom" but she's found her sparkle in writing about cannabis to inform, uplift, and occasionally challenge her readers while helping push the conversation forward. Her articles have appeared in numerous publications including The New York Times, The Week, Civilized, Vice, Double Blind, What's Up Moms, and Scary Mommy. She holds a BA from Dartmouth College and an MA from American University and has worked as a yoga teacher and trainer, a staff writer, and a researcher on issues of international conflict resolution. Danielle lives in the Northwest with her family and a very barky terrier.*

[1] Andrew J. Sun and Michael Eisenberg. "Association Between Marijuana Use and Sexual Frequency in The United States: A Population-Based Study," *The Journal of Sexual Medicine* 14, no. 11 (2017): 1342–1347, doi: 10.1016/j.jsxm.2017.09.005.

[2] Becky K. Lynn, et al. "The Relationship Between Marijuana Use Prior To Sex and Sexual Function in Women," *Sexual Medicine* 7 no. 2 (2019): 192–197, doi: 10.1016/j.esxm.2019.01.003121.

[3] Caroline Klein, et al. "Circulating Endocannabinoid Concentrations And Sexual Arousal In Women." *The Journal Of Sexual Medicine* 9 (6): 1588–1601. (2012) doi: 10.1111/j.1743-6109.2012.02708.x.

[4] Wei, Don, DaYeon Lee, Conor D. Cox, Carley A. Karsten, Olga Peñagarikano, Daniel H. Geschwind, Christine M. Gall, and Daniele Piomelli. 2015. "Endocannabinoid Signaling Mediates Oxytocin-Driven Social Reward." *Proceedings Of The National Academy Of Sciences* 112 (45): 14084-14089. doi:10.1073/pnas.1509795112.

Instructions: Take a break and ask yourself, would you rather:

☐

Your partner to tell you every day that you are sexy?

☐

Your partner to tell you every day that you are loved?

THIS OR THAT?

What made you choose your answer?

_____

_____

_____

_____

_____

_____

_____

_____

_____

_____

_____

_____

_____

_____

_____

_____

_____

_____

_____

_____

_____

_____

_____

_____

Make a connection. Take a picture and share with a loved one!

What do they think? Start a conversation.

After our marriage began to transform, I knew I didn't want to backslide, so I became fanatical about stopping any situation that felt reminiscent of our old patterns. Instead of the cordial "Complaint Department," the word I used for this was a bellowing, heard-throughout-the-house, "PAUSE!"

For the next week, when you want a conversation or situation to change, stop in the moment with your agreed-upon word. Don't worry if your words don't come out eloquently. The point is not to be right the first time or above reproach. The point is to be honest, and to create a new way of relating to each other in the situation. Let it be awkward, like you are rehearsing a play and trying to figure out your lines.

Remember that we all have some lines that need updating, so listen to your partner and play along.

Instructions: Brainstorm five of your own words for "pause" below. Agree on one with your partner. Reflect on what happened over the week. Write about how you felt and what shifted after you stopped in the moment.

LINE PLEASE

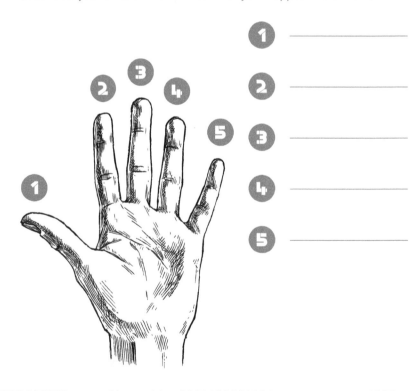

1 _____

2 _____

3 _____

4 _____

5 _____

Situation:

_____
_____
_____
_____

How I felt/what I feared:

_____
_____
_____
_____
_____
_____
_____
_____

How we shifted into a healthier dynamic:

_____
_____
_____
_____
_____
_____
_____
_____
_____
_____
_____

Situation:

_____

_____

_____

_____

How I felt/what I feared:

_____

_____

_____

_____

_____

_____

_____

_____

How we shifted into a healthier dynamic:

_____

_____

_____

_____

_____

_____

_____

_____

_____

_____

_____

_____

_____

_____

_____

Situation:

_____
_____
_____
_____

How I felt/what I feared:

_____
_____
_____
_____
_____
_____
_____
_____

How we shifted into a healthier dynamic:

_____
_____
_____
_____
_____
_____
_____
_____
_____
_____
_____
_____
_____
_____

Instructions: Sometimes it's hard to put your feelings into words. If you're feeling creative, try drawing them. This can be as expressive or symbolic as you like.

THIS IS HOW I FELT:

Make a connection. Take a picture and share with a loved one!

What do they think? Start a conversation.

Instructions: Draw what you feared would happen (worst case scenario is fine) or something that represents those fears.

THIS IS WHAT I FEARED:

Make a connection. Take a picture and share with a loved one!

What do they think? Start a conversation.

FROM *SWING*

When our kids were little, Manny used to play racquetball and go out for breakfast with his brothers every Sunday. It was the only day he didn't work, and he wanted to enjoy it. But I was pissed. I wanted a shirt that said, "Sunday Funday Can Kiss My Ass."

See, Sundays were my busiest day at work. All morning I would do last-minute practice planning while juggling three kids, then meet Manny in a random parking lot on the way to the rink to pass the children (including a nursing baby) off to him, then rush down to the rink. He'd then proceed to drop the kids off at his parents' house while he watched the football game at his brother's house.

I'd often tell him how upset it made me, and he felt super defensive. Didn't I want him to have any fun? Didn't I know his parents really wanted to see the kids?

Fuck all of that, really. All I wanted was to have just a little time to myself. So, I started to take it.

Around that time, I signed up for a mindful self-care program with my friends. Our facilitator was Sheila, who later became one of my best friends. Sheila instructed us to pick one small, doable thing to take better care of ourselves. I went very small and very simple. I decided to go pee when I needed to go pee.

I desperately wanted to tune into my body's deeper knowing and get more in touch with my intuition, but there I was, ignoring, sometimes for hours, one of my most basic needs. I decided on that day that whenever I felt I needed to go I would stop everything, turn off the stove, pause mid-conversation, and just go pee. Do not pass go. Do not collect $200. Just go pee.

Over the first few weeks I had the increasing awareness of just how often I ignored what my body was telling me. Whenever I would tell friends about it — because I thought it was revolutionary, and whenever I have an idea I think is good I shout it from the rooftops — their eyes would widen, and I could see them contemplating the opportunity in that simple action. And then almost all of them would tell me they simply could not do it. They were far too needed, far too busy to do something so indulgent. They were worried about what would happen to their kids, their jobs, their what-the-fuck-ever they were concerned about. Like everything would wilt and die and the world would stop turning if they actually took care of themselves for sixty fucking seconds.

They just couldn't do it. And most didn't. They feared that any type of self-care wasn't just indulgent, but potentially dangerous. Even with modern construction, reliable electricity, and our privileged lives, the simple truth remained. Most of us didn't feel safe unless we were putting ourselves last. I saw this in myself, taking on so much as a means of proving my worth, and the reflexive guilt I instantly felt if I put anyone's needs behind my own. As women, we had been putting the comfort of others over our own well-being generation after generation. We immediately felt unworthy or selfish if our needs were being met at all, because that signaled that someone else may be suffering. I saw it everywhere I looked, women putting themselves last and working themselves the hardest.

Need more room? Get half-price digital worksheets here.

THE LIFE CHANGING MAGIC OF PEEING WHEN YOU NEED TO PEE.

Make it your own. Color, write, or draw and share with our community!

@ashleighrenard | #KeepingItHot

Instructions: Pick one, small, doable thing you are going to do, starting today. Either write or draw that thing below.

I AM GOING TO START:

Make a connection. Take a picture and share with a loved one!

What do they think? Start a conversation.

If you had an hour how would you spend it? Who would you see, or not see? What would you do, or not do? What physical sensations would you savor?

Instructions: Write the first activities and people that come to mind. Check in with your body and notice what sensations would come up.

How would you spend your hour?

_____
_____
_____
_____

Who would you see, or not see in that hour?

_____
_____
_____
_____

What would you do, or not do in that hour?

_____
_____
_____
_____

What physical sensations would you savor?

_____
_____
_____
_____
_____

ONE HOUR

Instructions: Draw a scene from your hour. Try to capture how what you are doing and who you are with, or not with, is making you feel.

I WOULD SPEND AN HOUR:

Make a connection. Take a picture and share with a loved one!

What do they think? Start a conversation.

If you had a day how would you spend it? Who would you see, or not see? What would you do, or not do? What physical sensations would you savor?

Instructions: Write the first activities and people that come to mind. Check in with your body and notice what sensations would come up.

How would you spend your day?

_____
_____
_____
_____

Who would you see, or not see in that day?

_____
_____
_____
_____

What would you do, or not do in that day?

_____
_____
_____
_____

What physical sensations would you savor?

_____
_____
_____
_____
_____

ONE DAY

Instructions: Draw a scene from your day. Try to capture how what you are doing and who you are with, or not with, is making you feel.

I WOULD SPEND A DAY:

Make a connection. Take a picture and share with a loved one!

What do they think? Start a conversation.

If you had a week how would you spend it? Who would you see, or not see? What would you do, or not do? What physical sensations would you savor?

Instructions: Write the first activities and people that come to mind. Check in with your body and notice what sensations would come up.

How would you spend your week?

_____
_____
_____
_____

Who would you see, or not see in that week?

_____
_____
_____
_____

What would you do, or not do in that week?

_____
_____
_____
_____

What physical sensations would you savor?

_____
_____
_____
_____
_____

ONE WEEK

Instructions: Draw a scene from your week. Try to capture how what you are doing and who you are with, or not with, is making you feel.

I WOULD SPEND A WEEK:

Make a connection. Take a picture and share with a loved one!

What do they think? Start a conversation.

Instructions: Take a break and ask yourself, would you rather:

Play the role of dominant?

Play the role of submissive?

THIS OR THAT?

What made you choose your answer?

_____
_____
_____
_____
_____
_____
_____
_____
_____
_____
_____
_____
_____
_____
_____
_____
_____
_____
_____
_____
_____
_____
_____
_____

Make a connection. Take a picture and share with a loved one!

What do they think? Start a conversation.

Minus your immediate family (because we're stuck with those annoying buggers), think about the five people you spend the most time with.

Instructions: Write the name of the person and color in the gas gauges based on how much time you spend with them. After reflecting on your gas tank, use a check mark to indicate if you want to spend more or less time with each individual.

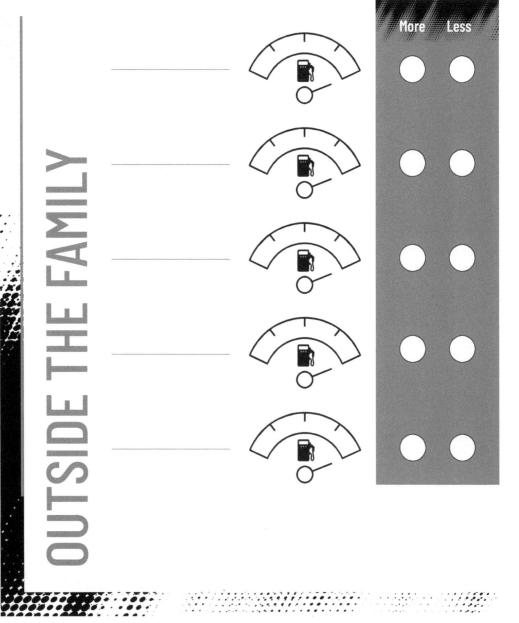

OUTSIDE THE FAMILY

Instructions: For the first person — if you want to spend more time with them, when will you do it? Where will you go? What will you do? What needs to happen to make it a date? If you want to spend less time with them, what needs to happen to reduce the time spent together? Write your thoughts down.

Before you say nothing, it's not possible, consider this..."You are the average of the five people you spend the most time with." - Jim Rohn

Instructions: For the second person — if you want to spend more time with them, when will you do it? Where will you go? What will you do? What needs to happen to make it a date? If you want to spend less time with them, what needs to happen to reduce the time spent together? Write your thoughts down.

Instructions: For the third person — if you want to spend more time with them, when will you do it? Where will you go? What will you do? What needs to happen to make it a date? If you want to spend less time with them, what needs to happen to reduce the time spent together? Write your thoughts down.

Instructions: For the fourth person — if you want to spend more time with them, when will you do it? Where will you go? What will you do? What needs to happen to make it a date? If you want to spend less time with them, what needs to happen to reduce the time spent together? Write your thoughts down.

Instructions: For the fifth person — if you want to spend more time with them, when will you do it? Where will you go? What will you do? What needs to happen to make it a date? If you want to spend less time with them, what needs to happen to reduce the time spent together? Write your thoughts down.

Now, considering family members as well, how full is your tank after spending an hour alone with each of them?

Instructions: Write the name of the person and color in the gas gauges below. After reflecting on your gas tank, use a check mark to indicate if you think their gas tank would look similar from their time with you.

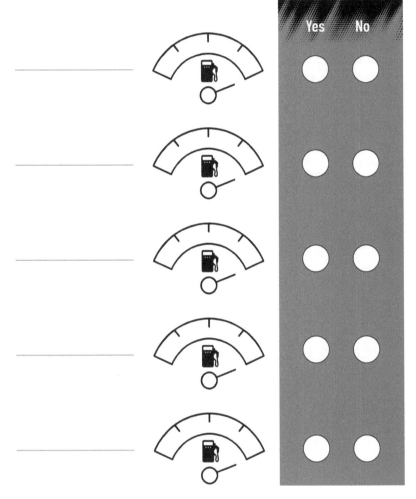

INSIDE THE FAMILY

Instructions: If you didn't answer yes, write down why you think that is. How does that make you feel? Is there anything realistic you can change with your time together so your time together makes your gas gauges feel similar?

_____

_____

_____

_____

_____

_____

_____

_____

_____

_____

_____

_____

_____

_____

_____

_____

_____

_____

_____

_____

_____

_____

_____

_____

_____

_____

_____

REMINDER: SPEND YOUR TIME WITH THE PEOPLE THAT FILL YOU UP.

Make it your own. Color, write, or draw and share with our community!

@ashleighrenard | #KeepingItHot

It's essential that we educate ourselves on experiences that differ from our own and use our privilege and resources to help make the world a better place. However, becoming overwhelmed by taking in too many streams of information is not a necessary part of this. We are going to revisit the gas tank exercise, this time focusing on media. For each media channel, ask yourself this question:

How educated, entertained, or inspired am I after spending an hour on this feed? How certain am I of the action I should take?

Instructions: Color in the gas gauge for each media channel below.

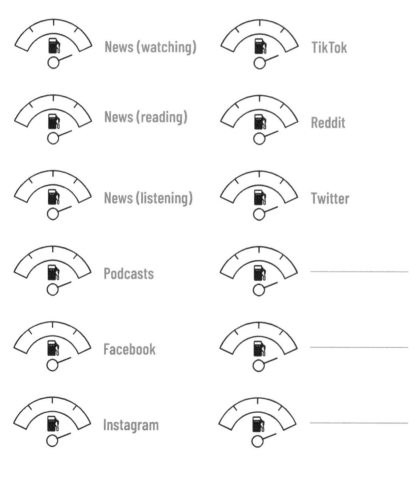

News (watching)

News (reading)

News (listening)

Podcasts

Facebook

Instagram

TikTok

Reddit

Twitter

MEDIA CHANNELS

Instructions: Reflect on your gas tanks for each media channel and answer the following questions.

What media sources do you want to make time for each day?

_____

_____

_____

_____

_____

How will you do this?

_____

_____

_____

_____

_____

What media sources do you want to engage with less?

_____

_____

_____

_____

_____

Ideas: Remove apps from your phone; fill the time with something else, like talking on the phone with a friend while walking; read a book on the train instead of scrolling on social media; learn a new language or use a meditation app for 30 minutes a day.

It is a great privilege to be able to turn away from the news and social media, but sometimes I just need to turn it all off for a few weeks and up my donations to the nonprofits I trust instead.

FROM *SWING*

Regardless of how loudly the big, beautiful human brain insists that it's running the show, either through outside teachings or inner knowings, many of us come to wonder if there is something deeper and broader animating and connecting us. Here is a snapshot of my fake-it-till-you-make-it approach to spirituality.

Until Jack was born, I believed that everything I needed to know could be explained by science. I was a skeptic raised by skeptics, a science-lover, and a logical decision maker. Soon after I became a mother, I realized that the world felt a little different. Well, a lot different. I didn't anticipate that along with a child, I would also birth an increased sensitivity to the energetic connection between all living things, past, present, and future. Sometimes I could even see it, a vibrating, reddish energy, linking all that is. Somehow, this tidbit was missed in my pregnancy books.

It filled me with a calm, a steadiness, quieting my mind in a way I had never experienced. At first, I didn't tell anyone, because it sort of weirded me out, and also because everyone around me knew that I rejected anything supernatural. It seemed hokey for me to announce to everyone, "Oh, yeah, you know that God thing that you've all been talking about? I get it now. All good." Because it wasn't all good. The experience was, but I had trouble reconciling it with what I had learned about God through religion.

Some kids grow up in religious homes and stash a *Playboy* under their mattress. I grew up in liberal home, and under my mattress was a bible. When I was little, I asked my parents questions about God, especially about how different people believed different things about God. My mom always said the same thing: "Whatever someone believes is right for them." And when I would continue to dig, she would say, "Please, Ashleigh, don't bother your [Catholic] Grandma with these questions."

From my Dad I heard, "Evolution, Ashleigh, I believe in evolution." He was a catechism dropout. And when I would persist, he'd say, "The monkeys, Ashleigh. I already told you, the monkeys."

I considered my town to be de facto Christian, since most kids I knew believed in Santa and the Easter Bunny. I knew very few families who were actually religious. But periodically at school, I would be passed a little comic book from one of my classmates who was a practicing Christian, always with the same hushed message: "I really like you, so I think you should know..." then their voice would trail off and off they would scamper. I'd flip to the second-to-last page and recoil, seeing the same thing as the time before, the little cartoon people burning in hell.

Clearly, I had no pressure to believe at home, but I could not shake the curiosity about why some people were so into religion. So, as soon as I started to drive, in addition to my secret bible studies, I became an undercover listener of Christian radio. For years, whenever I was alone in the car I would listen, then be certain to change to a different station before I got out. I kept it a secret to keep non-believers from thinking I would try to convert them and believers from seeing me as ripe for conversion. The truth was, even though I had these years of private contemplation, I still didn't feel convinced to buy in. Rather than experiencing the good news of the gospel, I felt I was being sold a pitch for a bad timeshare.

Christian Heaven Gatekeeper Timeshare Dude: Sign on the dotted line or you will regret it eternally. Yeah, it's not much now, but let me tell you about the upgrades coming in Phase 2. If you don't buy in now, you'll miss out on the eternity pool...

Me: Don't you mean the infinity pool?

Dude: No, an ETERNITY pool. It goes on FOREVER.

*Me: Uh, yeah...that's...okay, never mind. *Notices pervert jacking off in corner* Wait, what is going on with that guy??*

Dude: Ma'am, I'm going to have to ask you to cover your shoulders.

Not much of my secret bible study helped me make sense of my new spiritual awakening. I mostly kept it to myself and tried to just pay very close attention. Soon I started finding spiritual books, friends, and teachers who shared the same experience. Preparing for unmedicated birth and breastfeeding had linked me to a natural mom group. Within that community, I quickly found friends with rich experiences and understanding. Their belief was that our babies had chosen us as their families before birth, selecting parents who were best served to teach them the lessons they needed to learn during this lifetime.

Still pretty sure I was on an extended episode of *Punk'd*, I committed to reconciling my mothering exhaustion with my new spiritual awareness. I shared with my yoga teacher that I often felt that I needed the real mom to come home. I was not equipped to handle this. She replied confidently, "Well, you know you can handle this because you're a mama this time around."

I didn't know if I believed her, but I quickly realized that I felt better when I pretended I did. I felt calmer, more patient, and more content, basically an all-around better-functioning human being when I decided to pretend that I was put here on Earth, in my role, for a reason. It didn't matter if it was true or not. When I believed it, I felt more capable of dealing with the chaos. I felt like, *even if Ashton Kutcher never shows up, I've got this.*

And so began my fake it 'til you make it approach to spirituality.

What would happen if I sent a question out into the universe and trusted that I would get the right answer? What if I believed my intuition was linked to something broader, an intelligent energy that cared for me? I tested it out on both big and little decisions. Sometimes I would act on the answer I received; sometimes I wouldn't. Often, my fear prevented me from following through, but I found that my gut always told me the right thing to do. When I ignored it, the situation would intensify until I eventually let my intuition guide me.

I figured out that if I got quiet and listened, I would always know what to do. Even if everyone around me had an opinion, I could trust myself to have the answer. I became more confident, believing that this universal energy I sensed was intelligent and compassionate. I carefully chose words to explain what I was experiencing: first Prana, because I had experienced the surging of life force energy in yoga, then the Universe, the Divine, and then, after many, many years, God — but only with close friends who knew what I meant. "God" meant something very specific to most people, and it varied depending on their geography. In any case, I wanted to avoid using the word and having people jump to all sorts of conclusions about what else that meant about me. And just like people assumed (incorrectly) that I must be a vegetarian because I eat organic food and I kind of look like Dawn from The Babysitters' Club, their assumptions about what I meant by "God" and what else that meant about my views would likely be way off.

When I was pregnant with Niko, I found a lovely meditation teacher who said our experience of the Divine is similar to being blindfolded in a room with an elephant. Each one of us has our hand on a different part of the elephant: the tusk, the ear, the tail. And many of us insist that no one else is really touching the elephant unless they feel the same thing we do. *We are all connected to the same thing, she said, but experiencing it in different ways.*

I used to love to oversimplify. If I could distill a complicated set of ideas down to one blanket idea, I would. But I was shown over and over that when I expressed something with absolute certainty it turned out to be more nuanced than I had assumed. For this reason, whenever someone was absolutely certain of something, especially something related to God, I remained highly suspect of how much time they had actually spent listening to what the Divine wanted to teach them. I was certain that one of God's favorite games to play with me was, *believe this without doubt so I can spin you around and make you see it from the other side.*

My faith in my own eclectic blend of spirituality deepened. I came to believe that things in my life were happening *for* me, not just *to* me. Through consistent study, I came to appreciate that the physical world gives us many opportunities to work, play, and experience here, but the non-physical is what is real and unchanging. During my limited time at Earth School in my meat suit, I was going to try to be the best student. I looked for the deeper meaning in everything, including every time I dropped something or stubbed my toe.

Universe, what is it? I'm listening.

Ashleigh, you just stubbed your toe. It's nothing.

Are you sure I wasn't thinking about something that wasn't in my best interest and for the greater good of the world?

Nope. You just stubbed your toe.

Okay, just checking. Want to give me any other tidbits while we are here in conversation?

Drink more water.

Okay, Universe. Divine advice. Thank you.

Need more room? Get half-price digital worksheets here.

Instructions: Answer the following big questions. Dream big and be honest with yourself.

What books, teachers, or belief systems are you interested in that you haven't yet explored or would like to explore more deeply?

THE BIG QUESTIONS

How much time would you like to carve out for spiritual or grounding practices? Do you want to journal, meditate, walk in nature, or do breathwork?

Do you have a pull toward a passion that you have been ignoring?

Imagine you are living your ideal life. What does it look like? Are you in a different body? A different time? A different place?

Compare your life now to your dream scenario. What can you give yourself permission to want more of in your life right now?

_____

_____

_____

_____

_____

_____

_____

_____

_____

_____

_____

_____

_____

_____

_____

_____

_____

_____

_____

_____

_____

_____

_____

_____

What feelings come up when you consider giving yourself the permission you crave?

Instructions: Take a break and ask yourself, would you rather:

See a comedy show together?

Get an in-room couples massage at a hotel?

THIS OR THAT?

What made you choose your answer?

_____

_____

_____

_____

_____

_____

_____

_____

_____

_____

_____

_____

_____

_____

_____

_____

_____

_____

_____

_____

_____

_____

_____

Make a connection. Take a picture and share with a loved one!

What do they think? Start a conversation.

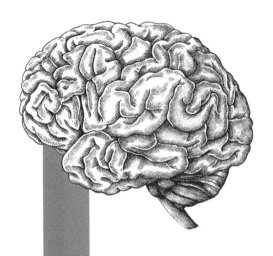

WHAT'S ON YOUR MIND?